The
Soviet Bloc,
Energy, and
Western
Security

The Soviet Bloc, Energy, and Western Security

Jonathan B. Stein
The Center for Strategic
and International Studies,
Georgetown University

Foreword by
Charles K. Ebinger

LexingtonBooks
D.C. Heath and Company
Lexington, Massachusetts
Toronto

Library of Congress Cataloging in Publication Data

Stein, Jonathan B.
  The Soviet bloc, energy, and western security.

  Includes index.
  1. Petroleum industry and trade—Political aspects—Soviet Union.
2. Petroleum industry and trade—Political aspects—Europe, Eastern.
3. Petroleum industry and trade—Political aspects—Arab countries.
4. Energy industries—Political aspects—Soviet Union. 5. Energy
industries—Political aspects—Europe, Eastern. 6. Energy
industries—Political aspects—Arab countries. 7. Soviet Union—Foreign
relations—Arab countries. 8. Europe, Eastern—Foreign relations—Arab
countries. 9. Arab countries—Foreign relations—Soviet Union. 10. Arab
countries—Foreign relations—Europe, Eastern. 11. World
politics—1975-1985. I. Title.
HD9575.S652S73   1983   327.1'11   82-24955
ISBN 0-669-06441-6

Published simultaneously in Canada

Printed in the United States of America

International Standard Book Number: 0-669-06441-6

Library of Congress Catalog Card Number: 82-24955

To my family

Contents

Figures and Tables

Foreword

This book is a pioneering work. From the first chapter, Jonathan Stein delineates in thorough detail the tough economic-policy decisions on energy confronting the Soviet Union and its East European allies. The choices are stark. In order to reduce the energy intensities of the bloc economies, Moscow must bring about either a marked improvement in energy-use efficiencies or a structural change away from fuels- and materials-intensive processes and sectors. In the first part of his book, Mr. Stein addresses the reasons why, in his expert opinion, the Soviet bloc does not have the capability or substantive willingness to effect such changes and what the implications of this indecision portend for both the East bloc and the West.

This book makes a valuable contribution to the literature on Soviet energy in that, by giving a thorough analysis of each energy source (oil, gas, coal, nuclear electricity, hydro, and renewables), Mr. Stein does what few other analysts have attempted: he concentrates on the entire energy sector and not just on oil. In the course of his examination, which benefits a great deal from reliance on primary Soviet source material (in translation), Mr. Stein adds new insights to the assessment of Soviet bureaucratic decision making in the energy sector. His observation that the Soviet government organs continue to support policies favoring the accelerated development of coal and nuclear power while the Communist party organs favor placing primary reliance on oil and gas follows Erik Jones's methodology while updating the ensuing debate in energy-policy formulation in the USSR.

The author's detailed delineation of how personnel shortages, lack of skilled drilling personnel, equipment shortages, low morale in the Arctic areas, and similar problems have impinged on Soviet energy development provides a sense of the magnitude of the problems confronting Moscow.

The analysis of the technical problems associated with Moscow's major oil fields reveals the difficult political and economic choices facing Soviet party and government leaders. As the author notes, a policy decision to continue to exceed the maximum economic recovery rate of the USSR's established giant and supergiant fields in West Siberia will seriously risk rapid depletion of the nation's best oil reservoirs. Such a decision would bring on an accelerated decline in the reserve-production ratio, leading to a rapid decline in oil production by the latter 1980s without sizable new additions to reserves. Clearly the geopolitical implications could be profound if, in the late 1980s, the USSR and Eastern Europe became major claimants to Middle Eastern oil supplies.

As Mr. Stein notes, however, even if Moscow pursues the opposite policy (pumping at a decelerated pace) to avoid the rapid decline in output, it will encounter intense political and economic difficulties as it is increasingly unable to satisfy domestic and East bloc consumption. Given Moscow's intense fears that political disturbances in Eastern Europe could multiply in the wake of deteriorating economic conditions, the author argues that Moscow will pursue a policy of overproduction of oil, hoping that a rapid development of coal and nuclear electricity and natural gas will alleviate bloc energy shortfalls later in the decade. The author's first-rate discussion of the legion of problems plaguing the coal and nuclear-power sectors, as well as his detailed examination of the consumption patterns of the East European economies, merit scrutiny by all serious analysts of the Soviet energy situation.

Perhaps the most-original contribution of this book is the analytical critique of the ongoing dispute between the Defense Intelligence Agency (DIA) and the Central Intelligence Agency (CIA) on the degree of seriousness of the Soviet energy dilemma. While others have subjected the various CIA analyses to close scrutiny, Mr. Stein's systematic examination of the assumptions behind the DIA assessment raises serious questions about the validity of the DIA's optimistic report. Perhaps most telling is the author's comment that he cannot understand why DIA consistently refers to the Salym oil reservoir as if it were a conventional field when in fact it is a shale-oil deposit plagued with far more developmental and technical problems than the far-richer oil-shale deposits found in the United States. Given that much of the DIA's assessment assumes that the Salym field will be producing in five to six years, one must question the entire validity of the DIA analysis. Mr. Stein's thorough analytical treatment of the DIA report adds an important new dimension to the Soviet energy debate.

Having shown the importance of energy in the economic and political future of the Soviet Council for Mutual Economic Assistance (CMEA), the author thoroughly delineates the controversy surrounding the construction of the Siberian gas pipeline and the implications for the West. Mr. Stein deserves praise for his balanced treatment of the varying U.S. and West European attitudes toward consummation of the pipeline deal. He elucidates the failure on both sides of the Atlantic to develop a common approach toward trade with the USSR and admonishes the allied community not to repeat past mistakes and effect a crash alliance policy to avoid divisive rancor in the future. The author warns that failure to address this issue risks perpetual conflict within the Western alliance.

One of the most-useful components of this book is its discussion of the future natural-gas market in Western Europe and the role that Soviet gas may play in meeting projected demand. The analysis of these issues must accompany any discussion of the controversial Soviet-pipeline project. The author dismisses the European view that the anticipated level of dependency on Soviet gas is not troublesome and queries whether the projected level of gas use in Italian industry and in the French and German residential and commercial sectors (coupled with the very high projected share of imports in total consumption) does not render all three nations subject to significant economic and political problems in the event of supply bottlenecks or cutoff. Mr. Stein is fair in noting the measures that Europeans are implementing to avoid such political blackmail.

This analysis concludes with positive recommendations on how the alliance can repair the discord engendered by the pipeline controversy. Mr. Stein raises questions about the institutional viability of NATO to meet the challenges posed by the East bloc's energy situation and warns that in the absence of a thorough examination of a number of other policy issues raised by the CMEA energy dilemma, the future of the West will be imperiled.

Charles K. Ebinger
The Center for Strategic and
International Studies,
Georgetown University

Acknowledgments

Working through a host of issues as complex as those covered in this book would not have been possible without the invaluable assistance and advice rendered by friends and colleagues. The research facilities and support afforded me by the Center for Strategic and International Studies (CSIS) enabled me to concentrate my efforts on the implications of Soviet-bloc energy development, for which I am deeply grateful. For this help, special thanks go to Dr. David M. Abshire, president of CSIS, and Dr. Amos A. Jordan, vice-chairman of CSIS.

I am particularly thankful to those Soviet specialists who participated in our February 1982 conference on Soviet energy prospects, especially Edward Hewett, Marshall Goldman, and Theodore Shabad. Their perspectives were most enlightening, and their contributions were greatly valued by all involved. I also thank Angela Stent, Robert Ebel, Bernard Kritzer, Martha Calwell-Harris, Jack Brougher, Fred Dorey, and Joseph Riva for their useful comments.

Finally, I am most thankful to my colleagues in the Energy Studies Program here at CSIS: Richard Kessler and Wayne Berman for their sage advice, Ellen P. Hall for her research assistance, and Pauline Younger for her ceaseless efforts in preparation of the manuscript.

I remain indebted to my program director, Charles Ebinger, whose thoughtful counsel, friendship, and support were generously extended and without which this study would not have been realized.

Abbreviations

mmbd	million barrels per day (of crude oil)
mmbdoe	million barrels per day of oil equivalent
bcm	billion cubic meters (of natural gas)
tcm	trillion cubic meters
b/d	barrels per day

Oil figures given in millions of tons are metric tons; approximately 50 million metric tons of annual crude-oil production or consumption equal 1 mmbd.

The
Soviet Bloc,
Energy, and
Western
Security

1

Energy and the
Soviet Economic Model

The economies of the European member-states of the Council for Mutual Economic Assistance (CMEA) share, among other distinct attributes, a high correlation between growth in energy inputs into their productive processes and the rate of annual economic growth.[1] The relationship between energy consumption and gross national product (GNP)—referred to as the energy-GNP ratio—aggregately measures the energy intensity of an economy. Coefficients of 1 or greater generally reflect inefficient energy performance, usually a constraint on economic growth.

Estimates of energy-GNP ratios over time in individual CMEA states have ranged from a low of 0.76 in the German Democratic Republic (GDR) to a high of 1.8 in Hungary and Bulgaria. Because of the great difficulties in accurately calculating economic variables in the Soviet Union and Eastern Europe, however, these and other statistics must be treated more as indications of trends rather than indisputable indexes. Nonetheless it is clear that in those states with ratios at 1 or above (all of the Soviet bloc save the GDR in most estimates, with the notable exception of the GDR estimate above 1 given in table 1-1) tremendous investment will be required to improve energy performance. In order to reduce the energy intensities of the bloc economies, either a marked improvement in utilization efficiency must be effected or a structural change must occur away from fuels- and materials-intensive processes and sectors.[2]

At present, the Soviet bloc does not exhibit a capability or willingness to make necessary changes. Investment in energy production and industrial infrastructure is routinely far less than that required to upgrade productivity and efficiency. In the current Soviet Five Year Plan (1981-1985), the ruble-equivalent of $42 billion was cut in early 1982 in capital construction and infrastructure investment, representing about one-twelfth of planned investment over the Five Year Plan (depending on the conversion of rubles to dollars). In February 1981, those funds were earmarked in part to help smooth the desirable transition from extensive to intensive growth through gains in labor and capital productivity. National campaigns aimed at conservation and elimination of waste have thus far proved of minor impact. Fuel switching to natural gas where applicable must await extensive pipe laying (because most new gas will move from northwest Siberia or Central Asia into the European regions) and costly boiler conversions. Substitution of coal for oil in the CMEA will increase the bloc's energy intensity:

1

Given the low quality of coal in power generation and the increased role of solid fuels for that purpose and boiler use as a whole in Soviet plans, increased electrification should lead to some acceleration in gross energy input.[3]

Oil is a dwindling resource in the Soviet bloc. Annual growth increments to oil production have significantly slowed and will show absolute declines later in the 1980s. Between 80 and 90 percent of Soviet reserves of oil, coal, natural gas, and hydroelectricity lie east of the Ural Mountains and the Caspian Sea, whereas 75 percent of the Soviet population, over 70 percent of electricity generation, and 80 percent of fuel consumption and industry are located west of the Urals in the European USSR.[4] The great expense involved in deep extraction and long-distance transport of Soviet energy resources (the costs associated with natural-gas transportation have tripled in recent years)[5] complicates economic planning and will worsen in the future as resource depletion and distances continue to grow.

The Stalinist mode of extensive economic growth, in which efficiency of operation was sacrificed to absolute growth in factor supply, has not been abandoned despite some organizational tinkering during the Khruschev years.[6] The heavy reliance on oil consumption by key productive sectors in conjunction with the extensive growth model indicates that less oil supplied to industry will result in lower economic growth rates unless there is timely substitution or improvements in efficiency.

Substitution (including nuclear power for electricity generation to cover peak demand in the European provinces and part of Eastern Europe) and greater efficiency will meet with continual delays or prove infeasible in many applications. Importation of energy technologies and equipment will be limited in their contribution to Soviet bloc output both by the lack of

Table 1-1
Energy Consumption per $1 GNP, 1978
(kg/Coal Equivalent)

Bulgaria	1.6
Czechoslovakia	1.6
German Democratic Republic	1.3
Hungary	1.0
Poland	1.5
Rumania	2.3
USSR	1.5
United States	1.2
Japan	0.5
Federal Republic of Germany	0.6

Source: Friedrich Levcik, "Czechoslovakia: Economic Performance in the Post-Reform Period and Prospects for the 1980s," in U.S. Congress, Joint Economic Committee, *East European Economic Assessment: Part 1—Country Studies, 1980* (February 27, 1981), p. 388.

hard currency, which will constrain large-scale acquisition, and by organizational impediments and grossly inadequate infrastructure, which will restrict the effectiveness of imported Western technology.

Not only did investment in Soviet coal and electricity projects fall during the Tenth Five Year Plan (1976-1980) but the efficiency of investment has been declining since the 1960s. In most of the CMEA, but especially in the Soviet Union, insufficient infrastructure and rising costs of extraction and transportation have largely contributed to the lowering of the output-capital ratio.[7] In the Soviet model, the capital stock determines both investment levels and gross output. A fall-off in the efficiency and productivity of investment and in the inputs into the growth of the capital stock can have no other effect but to cause an absolute decline in growth.

Problems of a structural nature will persist during the decade because of a deeply rooted systemic crisis in the CMEA economies. The crisis is at the same time political, social, and economic. The New Economic Mechanism in Hungary, heralded as a major departure in socialist economics, has proved an innovative experiment, but it cannot escape the theoretical strictures imposed by Marxist-Leninist political doctrine or most of the adverse effects flowing from the application of socialist organization.

Overbureaucratization and centralized planning have been strapped onto an inherently inefficient, wasteful, and incentives-devoid economic structure in the CMEA system. Competition is choked off because of the state's allocation system and the tight control over the free flow of regional factors of production and international trade. The planning process in the CMEA is not a monolith, but there are several noteworthy characteristics shared by the member-states. The first and foremost structural imperative, virtually an immutable law of CMEA planning, is the stress on heavy industry.

Heavy-industrial development is energy and capital intensive at both the construction phase and throughout the operational life of new plants and equipment.[8] Without a constantly growing raw materials and energy supply, the heavy-industry sectors will not meet their targets with the predictable fall in economic growth. The principal obstacle for East European nations is the slowed growth of energy and natural-resource inputs from bloc sources at less than world market prices; imports of requisite materials from Organization of Economic Cooperation and Development (OECD) sources require hard currency—conspicuously lacking in the CMEA—or further indebtedness, which none of the satellites can now afford even if they could acquire additional loans or guarantees from Western banks and governments, an uncertain prospect given the Polish and Rumanian debt crises.

A second problem common to all bloc economies is the pressure to meet or overfulfill the plan. Gross output indicators are the arbiters of success for middle- and upper-level factory managers and bureaucrats. The emphasis on output inexorably leads to waste and expanded use of inputs, while simultaneously curbing innovation for fear of missing the plan. This ties in to the problems inherent in centralized bureaucratic control, which cannot be reformed away or made more rational in the Soviet bloc for evident historical reasons, in particular the region's postwar political development. As Thad P. Alton has pointed out:

> Bureaucracies do not die easily; on the contrary they seem to regroup and expand. In Eastern Europe where the hegemony of the Communist Party is held inviolate, it will be difficult to allow extensive freedom to managers, technocrats, and workers for fear of challenge to this principle.[9]

A third component of the CMEA system, not codified in organic bylaws but growing in practice, is the heavy reliance of Eastern Europe and the non-European allies on Soviet subsidies. Less than $2 billion of Soviet aid and subsidies, including the opportunity cost of supplying oil exports to the bloc at much less than world prices, was disbursed to the CMEA in 1971; this figure rose to $24 billion (most of which went to Eastern Europe) in 1980.[10] With its economic growth slowing in the early 1980s, the USSR will have increasing difficulty in rendering ever-growing subsidies to the bloc. Yet the political imperative of providing such assistance will not diminish. The move toward political and economic democratization in Poland in 1980-1981 may not be as contagious as many in the West would have hoped, but Moscow cannot gamble on the ultimate consequences of another bloc economic crisis.

In fact, the suppression of Polish dissent through the crackdown on Solidarity in December 1981 cannot be dismissed as the final episode in that struggle. Resistance, either violent or passive, could persist for years. A sharp decline in economic growth in Hungary or Czechoslovakia could unleash hostilities, pent up for years, toward the control mechanisms in place.

The Soviet economic model as applied in Eastern Europe will not only be plagued, as in the past, by accumulated stresses and strains caused by associated inefficiencies; it will also encounter a popular labor-based unrest. Reports of work stoppages and attempts at free trade-union organization have been cited throughout Eastern Europe and in the Soviet Union itself. The Ukraine (the Donetsk coal basin region), Kiev, the Baltic region, Tallinn, Naberezhnoye Cheleny, Togliatti, and Gorki have witnessed recent worker unrest, and the Soviet government has thus far shown more inclination to accommodate worker demands—probably as a result of the limited nature of those demands—than to crush worker opposition.

The rising indebtedness of the bloc, estimated in April 1982 at over $80 billion, including the Soviet Union, does not augur well for economic performance in the 1980s. Declining oil production in the USSR will force the

Soviets to decide between oil exports to the West for hard currency and oil exports to Eastern Europe for political expediency.

Should Moscow test its allies and cut Eastern Europe's oil deliveries by half the 1981 levels (about 1.6 mmbd, or 80 million tons), annual growth at mid-decade would decline by 1.4 percent in Bulgaria, 1 percent in Czechoslovakia, 1.3 percent in the GDR, and 1.2 percent in Hungary compared to what that growth would have been were Soviet oil exports to continue at 1980 levels.[11] The effects on Poland and Rumania would be negligible according to this estimate, but Polish sensitivity to Soviet oil will probably grow as Polish coal production falters or fails to increase in the years ahead.

In these growth estimates, the average growth rates under consideration are not very large even under an optimistic oil-supply scenario. Debt-service ratios ranging from over 20 percent in Czechoslovakia to at least 90 percent in Poland will hinder CMEA efforts to acquire hard currency through a rapid export-promotion policy, which could cover bloc requirements for world oil purchases. Imports of advanced technology and quality equipment from OECD states, which would upgrade CMEA's ability to export to the West, will be limited by the bloc's lack of hard currency; availability of Western credits and loans has already tightened and will certainly be more difficult to arrange in the future.

The energy-intensity coefficient is directly related to the level of CMEA debt and hard-currency import capacity. If fuel-substitution possibilities are limited as I believe they are to at least 1985, then an improvement in the energy-GNP ratio will rest largely on progress made in efficiencies of production. In this sphere, positive gains are doubtful:

> Especially low rates of capital stock retirement in Eastern Europe coupled with an expected slowdown of productive investment seem to define a fairly predictable short term picture for growth of capital stock. . . . Moreover, one doubts that the existing output mix will shift very much.[12]

Obsolete and inefficient energy-intensive equipment and processes, then, will continue to dominate industrial production in the CMEA. The bloc is predisposed both toward heavy industries and extensive growth, which together with centralized economic management and tight party control, result in an entrenched bureaucratic system. In this context, change by meaningful reform is unlikely. The high correlation between energy growth and economic modernization and development will remain strong in the CMEA for the rest of the 1980s.

Notes

1. The organization is also known as COMECON but will be referred to here as CMEA with focus on the Warsaw Pact members: the USSR,

Bulgaria, Czechoslovakia, the German Democratic Republic, Hungary, Poland, and Rumania. Non-European members include Cuba, Mongolia, and Vietnam. Yugoslavia holds associate membership; "non-socialist cooperant status" has been extended to Finland, Iraq, and Mexico. Observer status is held by Afghanistan, Angola, Cambodia, Ethiopia, Mozambique, and South Yemen. Paul Marer and John Michael Montias, "CMEA Integration: Theory and Practice," U.S. Congress, Joint Economic Committee, *East European Economic Assessment: Part 2—Regional Assessments* (July 10, 1981), pp. 149-150 (hereafter referred to as JEC(1).)

2. Leslie Dienes, "Energy Conservation in the USSR," in U.S. Congress, Joint Economic Committee, *Energy in Soviet Policy* (June 11, 1981), p. 103. The estimates of energy-GNP ratios are taken from U.S. Congress, Office of Technology Assessment, *Technology and Soviet Energy Availability* (November 1981), p. 301, and Jonathan P. Stern, *East European Energy and East-West Energy Trade* (London: Policy Studies Institute, 1982), p. 35.

3. Dienes, "Energy Conservation," p. 105.

4. Major Russell V. Olson, Jr., and William H. Berentsen, "Regional Energy Accessibility in the USSR," *Soviet Geography* (March 1981):135, and V. Voropaeva and S. Litvak, "The Fuel and Energy Balance of the USSR," *Soviet Law and Government* (Fall 1978):78. The strains caused by the vast distances between producing and consuming regions were recently alluded to by A. Alexandrov, president of the Soviet Academy of Sciences. "Soviet Western Sector Said to Face Problems as Fuel Supply Shrinks," *Wall Street Journal*, June 2, 1981, p. 34.

5. Major General Richard X. Larkin and Edward M. Collins, Defense Intelligence Agency, Statement before the Joint Economic Committee, Subcommittee on International Trade, Finance, and Security Economics, *Allocation of Resources in the Soviet Union and China—1981*, July 8, 1981, p. 22.

6. R.T. Maddock, "Oil and Economic Growth in the Soviet Union," *Three Banks Review* (March 1980):28-29. "Factor supply" here refers to the traditional factors of production: land, labor, and capital.

7. DIA, *Allocation of Resources*, p. 23.

8. Paul Marer, "Economic Performance and Prospects in Eastern Europe: Analytical Summary and Interpretation of Findings," JEC(1), p. 42.

9. Thad P. Alton, "Production and Resource Allocation in Eastern Europe: Performance, Problems, and Prospects," in JEC(1).

10. DIA, *Allocation of Resources*, p. 10.

11. Robin A. Watson, "The Linkage between Energy and Growth Prospects in Eastern Europe," in JEC(1), p. 499.

12. Ibid., p. 502.

2 Soviet Oil Prospects to 1990

In 1977 the Central Intelligence Agency (CIA) released three "pessimistic" research reports reversing the agency's earlier thinking on Soviet oil production.[1] In response, a spate of Western articles and books appeared both supporting and refuting the CIA's methodology and conclusions. Among the more-prominent refutations of the new CIA position were the Defense Intelligence Agency (DIA) prepared statements before the Joint Economic Committee of Congress; additionally, many private scholars have contributed to what has become a running debate on the future of Soviet oil and energy production.

Analyzing USSR oil production is made particularly difficult by the Soviet refusal to publish oil-reserve figures, a state secret for thirty-six years. Without reasonably accurate reserve figures, assessing the reserves-to-production ratio becomes a guessing game; an important index for measuring future production possibilities is thereby subject to great uncertainty. The problem posed by the wide divergence in Western reserves estimates is further compounded by the CIA's subsequent hedging of its 1977 pessimistic forecasts: first in April 1980 and then again in the spring of 1981.

Nevertheless, some assessment can be made within the range of various projections. Informed geological and economic estimates of reserves probabilities and reserves-to-production ratios and output trends are offered in this chapter. Remaining chapters examine CMEA energy and hard-currency problems, alternatives to oil production and consumption, and the geopolitical implications of Soviet fuels development and trade with Western Europe.

Oil Prospects

The CIA-DIA dispute over Soviet oil and energy forecasting is but one of many public disagreements in the field of estimating future Soviet-bloc energy availability. Divergent estimates serve institutional biases. Thus, if one posits a Soviet thrust into the Persian Gulf, the pessimistic CIA reports help drive one's conclusions. Simiarly, more-sanguine institutional thinking concerning evolving Soviet Middle East policy intentions tends to rely for support on optimistic forecasts from such authoritative sources as the DIA. Interestingly Secretary of Defense Caspar Weinberger in testimony before the Congress appears to have accepted the CIA's belief that the Soviets are experiencing many production difficulties, leaving his own intelligence agency dangling without firm cabinet support.

As the principal hard-currency earner and as a potential arbiter of Soviet foreign-policy decision making, oil production and therefore oil-export availability deserve special analysis for the determination of the proper U.S. and NATO response. At least until the mid-1980s, oil production will be central to Soviet foreign-exchange earnings, after which natural-gas exports via the Siberian pipeline project are scheduled to approach and eventually surpass oil earnings (as oil exports are phased out).[2]

Reserves

Proven oil-reserves estimates range from a 1977 and 1979 CIA figure of 33 billion barrels of oil to a 1979 (Swedish) PetroStudies figure of 150.27 billion barrels.[3] Jonathan Stern, in a compendium of essays published by the U.S. Congress in June 1981, has collected a number of Western reserves estimates and found that a mid-range of 60.1 billion to 75.5 billion barrels of proven oil reserves is considered most likely by U.S. and European specialists.[4] These estimates are about twice the level of U.S. proven reserves (29 billion to 30 billion barrels).

As much as half or more of the proven reserves are thought to lie in West Siberia, a region that accounted for 55 percent of All-Union production in 1981.[5] This percentage will undoubtedly increase by 1990 as older producing regions west of the Ural Mountains dry up and newer producing regions (Komi Autonomous Soviet Socialist Republic (ASSR), East Siberia, the North Caucasus, and Lesser Caucasus belts), currently of minor national importance, remain small producers compared with the giant and supergiant West Siberian reservoirs.[6]

Several noteworthy reserves discussions deserve mention. B.A. Rahmer of *Petroleum Economist* has noted that while 70 billion to 75 billion barrels of oil may be assumed to exist, over half of these reserves remain "to be definitely proven."[7] If the figures are accurate, then current production levels of 12.2 mmbd would grant between eight and sixteen more years of oil production at 1981 levels, depending on how quickly probable reserves are upgraded to proven reserves. Oil production will not then be able to sustain the high annual output of recent years. Unless new additions to reserves equal to yearly production are proved up each year, output will be forced downward if the Soviets desire a smooth rather than a rapid decline.

The eleventh Soviet Five Year Plan, officially released at the Twenty-sixth Party Congress in February 1981, called for a 1985 oil target of 12.4 to

12.9 mmbd, which has since been revised to 12.6 mmbd or 630 million tons. Some observers, apparently calculating a lower proven reserve base than the averaged Western estimates, have noted with concern the long lead times necessary to develop new energy sources. Assuming that no significant oil reservoirs have been discovered and developed since 1973—and there is no firm evidence to the contrary—oil production could well decline by an average of 300,000 b/d each year between 1986 and 1989.[8] This would leave end-of-decade production at 11 mmbd, a drop of 1.2 mmbd from current output.

In a recent study, Arthur A. Meyerhoff, a petroleum consultant with extensive experience in Soviet oil analysis, has placed the proven oil reserve base at 43.5 billion barrels.[9] Having surveyed recent Soviet literature, Meyerhoff claims there is evidence that the reserves-to-production ratio has slipped to a low of six-to-one. With 1981 production just over 4.4 billion barrels, however, proven reserves could be as low as 26.4 billion barrels. An unpublished 1974 Soviet Ministry of the Petroleum Industry study suggested that oil output could begin to slide by 1982, based on very low reserves indexes close to the figure of 26 billion barrels. Examination of Soviet reserves estimates and current production, therefore, leads Meyerhoff to conclude "that the U.S.S.R. will be entering the world market some 2 to 5 years after 1985."

Along these lines, Joseph P. Riva, Jr., a geologist with the Congressional Research Service, has placed the proven reserve base at a higher level of 58 billion barrels. This figure has remained constant since 1970, however; yearly additions to reserves have averaged 3.6 billion barrels. This annual reserves-addition rate was outpaced by annual production in the latter 1970s; thus, "increases in Soviet production were largely derived from the decrease in the reserves/production ratio." In order to maintain stable production in the 1980s at a reserves-to-production ratio of thirteen-to-one (the ratio applicable to 1980-1981 output if reserves are estimated at 58 billion barrels), additions to reserves must average 20 percent per year more than comparable 1970s additions. Forty-four billion barrels, 8 billion more than were discovered in the 1970s, must be added to reserves; a complicating factor will be the decline in the oil-discovery rate per foot drilled. Should the Soviets continue producing at current volumes, without the necessary reserves additions, they risk lowering the reserves-to-production ratio below ten-to-one, which would hasten the ultimate decline of the reservoir.[10] (If Meyerhoff is correct in his reserves estimates, then an *irreversible* production decline must come about within several years.)

In November 1981, the Congressional Office of Technology Assessment (OTA) published *Technology and Soviet Energy Availability*. Reference to exploration and reserves is instructive in that noted gaps in quantity and quality of seismic exploration equipment are related to the lack of incentives for increased exploratory effort inherent in the Soviet energy system. Greater allocations of resources toward exploration resulting in more feet drilled per year will not guarantee significant new finds. OTA believes, however, that the differences between Western and Soviet reserves definitions and categories, coupled with the uncertain nature of estimating reserves in absentia, make reserves assumptions too tenuous to predict firmly. However, OTA does not share CIA's pessimism concerning current reserve levels or additions to reserves.[11]

Finally, the CIA and DIA have greatly divergent estimates of Soviet oil reserves. The CIA has not publicly changed its 1977 assertion that Soviet proven oil reserves are approximately 33 billion barrels, whereas the DIA has upgraded its 1977 estimate of 75 billion barrels to 80 billion to 85 billion barrels. Of this, DIA believes that West Siberia retains 40 billion to 45 billion barrels, half their total All-Union estimate. The higher DIA reserves projection is but one of several factors cited by the DIA in support of the belief that Soviet oil production will continue to edge upward throughout the 1980s.[12]

Output Trends

Oil output in the USSR increased 0.7 percent between 1980 and 1981, and preliminary estimates indicate growth of about 0.4 percent between 1981 and 1982. What do past trends tell us about future production? Can the Soviet Union achieve the revised plan, or must Gosplan (the State Planning Commission) prepare the leadership for negative-production growth rates?

As table 2-1 indicates, the two most important oil provinces in the Soviet Union are West Siberia and the Urals-Volga. Three facts are apparent. First, Urals-Volga production peaked in 1975, and the pace of decline has been accelerating since 1976. Second, West Siberian production must therefore produce at an increased daily rate sufficient to offset Urals-Volga declines. Data for 1981, however, indicate that the rate of increase in West Siberian production fell by more than one-third (as against the performance of the mid-to-late 1970s).[13] An estimated 380,000 b/d (19 million tons) were natural-gas liquids in 1980.[14] This percentage has risen steadily at least since 1975 and current trends point to a continued increase. Third, production from the eight remaining oil regions has registered either small gains, remained stable, or diminished.

West Siberia

The failure to conduct adequate exploratory drilling in the USSR's most-prolific oil province helps explain the recent downturn in West Siberian

Table 2-1
Regional Production of Crude Oil, USSR
(million b/d)

	1970	1971	1972	1973	1974	1975	1976	1977	1978	1979	1980ᵃ
Total	**7.06**	**7.54**	**8.01**	**8.58**	**9.18**	**9.82**	**10.39**	**10.92**	**11.43**	**11.71**	**12.03**
Urals-Volga	4.17	4.23	4.32	4.43	4.46	4.52	4.51	4.42	4.29	4.03	3.82
West Siberia	0.63	0.90	1.25	1.75	2.33	2.96	3.63	4.37	5.08	5.66	6.25
Central Asia	0.60	0.68	0.73	−0.78	0.80	0.83	0.80	0.71	0.63	0.60	0.57
Azerbaijan SSR	0.40	0.38	0.37	0.36	0.35	0.34	0.33	0.31	0.30	0.29	0.28
North Caucasus	0.70	0.74	0.71	0.61	0.56	0.47	0.44	0.44	0.43	0.42	0.40
Ukrainian SSR	0.28	0.29	0.29	0.28	0.27	0.26	0.23	0.21	0.19	0.17	0.16
Komi ASSR	0.15	0.16	0.17	0.18	0.20	0.22	0.26	0.29	0.34	0.38	0.37
Belorussia SSR and Baltic	0.08	0.11	0.12	0.14	0.16	0.16	0.12	0.10	0.08	0.06	0.06
Far East	0.05	0.05	0.05	0.05	0.05	0.05	0.05	0.04	0.04	0.05	0.06
Georgian SSR	Negl.	Negl.	Negl.	Negl.	Negl.	0.01	0.02	0.03	0.05	0.05	0.06

Source: CIA, "International Energy Statistical Review," January 26, 1982, p. 24.

Note: Including natural-gas liquids.

ᵃPreliminary.

production increases. We can see from Figure 2-1 that the region's important oil districts are Tyumen Oblast and Tomsk Oblast, Tyumen being by far the more productive. Within Tyumen, nineteen giant and supergiant oil fields contributed the bulk of Tyumen production.

In 1981, West Siberian output averaged 6.68 mmbd (334 million tons per year), just under 55 percent of total Soviet output. Of this, the supergiant Samotlor field (estimated reserves of 14.6 billion barrels) contributed over 3 mmbd, one-quarter of all Soviet production. Much attention has therefore been paid to Samotlor. Whether it has peaked and how long it can hold at peak levels has been the subject of much speculation in the West.[15]

The West Siberian and Kara Sea basins, an area of 2.1 million square miles, are estimated by the U.S. Geological Survey (USGS) to contain 35 billion barrels of "demonstrated" reserves and an additional 30 billion barrels of "inferred" reserves.[16] Recent exploratory efforts have shifted northward from the Middle Ob' River Valley, where Samotlor, Fedorovo (possible reserves of 2 billion barrels), and other Tyumen giants granted the USSR yearly production gains.

As exploration and development shift away from the largest and most-accessible structures, costs have increased and more exploratory (as against development) drilling must be undertaken. In 1979, of the 19.75 million feet of West Siberian drilling achieved, 17.25 million feet went toward development drilling and only 2.5 million feet went toward exploratory drilling.[17] In order to stabilize output at current high levels, it is probable that the ratio of development to exploratory drilling in West Siberia will not be significantly altered. This does not bode well given the declining discovery rate.

Critics of the CIA and other pessimistic oil-forecast studies have stressed the existence of the vast stretches of Siberian territory, West and East, which they claim contain enormous hydrocarbon potential.[18] Three resource-based arguments, however, indicate that the size or petroleum potential of Siberia will not substantially alter the 1980s production horizon.

The first problem relates to the geographical areas of future exploration. As exploratory drilling spreads north and east, the coincidence of gas-prone basins will steadily increase. The USGS notes that "gas will be concentrated in the northern region of the assessment area because of presence of permafrost seal."[19] Not only will more of the basin's natural gas be discovered farther north, but the oil trapped in the northern reaches will be quite deep and difficult to recover. Tomsk and Novosibirsk, two areas often touted as giant-prone oil regions, are characterized by Paleozoic formations. But while "upper Paleozoic units are prospective . . . they are not expected to be significant, in part owing to erratic distribution."[20] In other

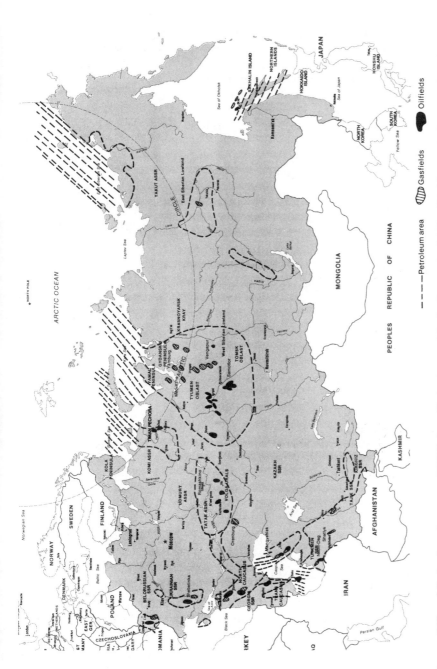

Source: Office of Technology Assessment (OTA), from *Technology and Soviet Energy Availability*, Washington, D.C., November 1981, p. 21.

Figure 2-1. Major Petroleum Basins, Oil Fields, and Gas Fields, USSR

words, the oil found in Paleozoic formations in these basins will only prove of marginal national importance. Finally, while the possibility exists of adding to reserves and production in the central and southern districts of West Siberia—and here the most-likely candidate for expansion would be the giant Fedorovo field—the westerly location of Federovo and similar fields argues against undue optimism in this regard.[21]

The second analysis supports the contention that the West Siberian discovery rate has sharply declined. The hydrocarbon reservoirs already discovered in the region are scattered over 400,000 square miles, a substantial portion of the area's sedimentary rock distribution (a range of over 700,000 square miles to 1.6 million square miles). "As a general rule outside the U.S.S.R., when that much of an area has been at least partly explored the remaining area is far less productive than the partly explored area."[22] Given the lead times necessary to bring new discoveries on stream in Arctic or sub-Arctic climes, current exploration must yield significant finds if the 1980s will witness production stabilization or gains.

A third analysis examined the USGS 1977 basin analogue of the West Siberian basin. West Siberia is classified as a Cratonic Type 2 (composite or 2A) Complex basin. The average yield for a basin of this nature is 100,000 barrels of oil per cubic mile of sediment; about 65 percent of the hydrocarbon yield in this type of basin is expected to be natural gas. Typical as well is a balance between giant and nongiant fields after some amount of development. The nongiant smaller fields can thus be expected to predominate in future discoveries, driving up the costs of extraction and limiting the size of yields.

If we accept the 1977 USGS estimate of 80 billion barrels of recoverable oil in West Siberia and if 37 billion barrels have been produced to date, then the remaining 43 billion barrels will approximate the additions to reserves necessary to maintain ouput in the 1980s at the thirteen-to-one reserves-to-production ratio. "Since this oil is more likely to be found in non-giant fields than in giants and since non-giants take more time to discover and exploit, it is doubtful that the West Siberia basin can be counted on to stabilize production."[23]

Several other factors must be included in any discussion of West Siberia's prospects. I. Korostelev, an engineer from Surgut, recently declared that the average yield per new well within West Siberia would decline from 93 metric tons per day in the 1976-1980 period to 38 metric tons per day in the 1981-1985 period.[24] About 75 percent of the territory is swampy, and lakes cover an additional 10 percent. Construction of railroads and highways is difficult and expensive and must cross broad-river floodplains, requiring new bridges, dikes, and drainage systems.[25]

In the Nizhnevartovsk district of Tyumen Oblast, within which lies Samotlor, the swampy conditions reinforce the inaccessibility by road of ten of the fifteen producing fields. No relief is expected soon.[26] Part of the problem in the Eleventh Five Year Plan stems from the northward direction of future drilling.

The 1982 exploratory and developmental drilling targets given by the Ministry of the Petroleum Industry are 44.6 million feet for West Siberia, an increase of 23 percent over 1981 drilling; A. Lalayants, the deputy chairman of Gosplan, has announced that 1981-1985 development drilling will total 249.5 million feet, an increase of 88.8 million feet above the Tenth Five Year Plan.[27] The drilling costs will increase correspondingly from about 200 rubles per meter in the Middle Ob' district of Tyumen to 500 rubles per meter at the Arctic Circle to 1,600 rubles per meter above the Arctic Circle. Infrastructural costs—roads, rail, housing, schools, communications, and service facilities—will similarly escalate.[28] If, as expected, Tyumen's three largest fields peak by 1985—Samotlor, Fedorovo, and Mamontovo (providing 61 percent of 1981 West Siberian output)—then less money will be available for northern and eastern construction and drilling because of the large expenditures necessary to stabilize production.[29]

The current plan projects West Siberian production of 7.7 to 7.9 mmbd in 1985 and 10 mmbd by 1990. Importation of sophisticated drilling technology is required if the planned 33 million feet of exploratory drilling during the Eleventh Five Year Plan will be accomplished. This must be achieved within the constraints of a dwindling number of serviceable rigs and turbodrills and drill bits manufactured domestically.[30] While the depths of penetration have increased, rig productivity (feet drilled per rig) has decreased as Soviet equipment proves increasingly incapable of sustained deep drilling.

The Soviet press, apparently divided in their loyalties (the party group formerly led by Brezhnev and now by Andropov and reflected in *Pravda* usually favors oil and gas development, whereas the government people, formerly led by Kosygin and now by N. Tikhonov, use *Izvestia* to push coal and nuclear), has not been shy in pointing to regional difficulties.[31] *Izvestia,* for example, has recently suggested that oil consumption is too high and that not enough petroleum is recovered from existing deposits.[32]

Soviet press comment concerning Tyumen, however, cannot be so readily broken down. *Pravda* of November 14, 1980, states that the equipment in use is so unreliable that 30 percent of Tyumen employees spend their time repairing and servicing equipment, facilities, and installations. About 400,000 extra workers will be required over the next few years in order to fulfill drilling-brigade needs.[33] If personnel shortages, low productivity, and thoroughly inadequate housing and services infrastructure continue to plague Tyumen (especially north Tyumen) operations, even the "flying-team" method of temporarily abating skilled labor shortfalls by flying in oil (and gas) teams from European regions may prove insufficient or too costly.

An *Izvestia* story of September 27, 1980, chronicles a shortfall in the Nizhnevartovsk district's construction of operational wells "by more than 337,000 meters—approximately 160 wells." Nizhnevartovsk is responsible for the majority of Tyumen oil production. *Izvestia* further complains that one of four wells is idle at a typical Soviet field and that the Ministry of Transport Construction "has obstinately resisted developing its capacity in the northern part of the province."[34]

Expansion of known fields through infill drilling at a deposit's margins appears to be Moscow's plan to maintain high production in the West Siberian basin. Although it is difficult, if not impossible, to gauge future success in this endeavor, adverse trends in the discovery rate coupled with the larger number of smaller pools that will have to be brought into production quickly should be cause for concern at Gosplan. The shale oil Salym field will not produce more than 5 million tons per year (100,000 b/d) beginning in 1986.[35]

If West Siberia cannot increase its 1985 production to 385 million to 395 million tons per year (7.7 to 7.9 mmbd) or, achieving 1985 plan targets, hold that level throughout the remainder of the decade, then the goals for non-West Siberian output take on significantly greater importance.

Urals-Volga and Remaining Regions

Siberia, Komi, the North Caucasus, and the Urals-Volga regions comprise the oil-producing districts of the Russian Socialist Federated Soviet Republic (RSFSR). In 1981 the RSFSR output was slightly over 11 mmbd. The expectation is for 1985 RSFSR production to total 11.4 mmbd and for non-RSFSR production (Central Asia, the Ukraine, Georgia, Azerbaijan, Belorussia, Kazakhstan, and Turkmenia) to total 1.2 mmbd. Thus, RSFSR output is scheduled to climb by 400,000 b/d, while non-RSFSR output is slated only for an additional 100,000 b/d. Clearly production targets outside West Siberia must be met if All-Union output is to rise or remain steady.

The Urals-Volga petroleum basin, long the mainstay in Soviet oil efforts and now in decline, covers an area of 190,000 square miles. Demonstrated reserves are estimated at 5 billion barrels and inferred reserves at 5 billion barrels. The USGS notes that "significant new plays are not likely in the area."[36] The province's output has dropped over 600,000 b/d since 1975 and is expected to decline an additional 1.1 mmbd by 1985 (to a total production level of 2.7 mmbd).[37]

The Urals-Volga province enabled the Soviet Union to become an oil exporter. The supergiant Romashkino provided about 35 percent of Urals-

Volga oil; the province peaked in twenty-five years (in 1975) with Romashkino accounting for 76 percent of regional production in that year.[38]

Table 2-2 displays the gains and losses registered in the non-Siberian oil basins since 1975. While Komi, Udmurt, Kaliningrad, and Georgia have grown by 299,000 b/d, the other producers have declined by 1.63 mmbd. The future growth potential of those areas registering gains is uncertain. Komi is expected to raise production about 70,000 b/d by 1985. The Timan-Pechora complex (Komi's principal energy basin), however, suffers from a lack of water lines for continuous water injection, too few modular construction units, poor roads that make passage to the drilling sites impossible on many days, and a lack of exploratory drilling.[39]

The water-injection process, necessary to restore well pressure, eventually degrades output. The Urals-Volga and West Siberian fields have both experienced rising water content in recent years, surpassing 50 percent of the liquids extracted in many fields. In all probability Komi will not be an exception to the near-universal Soviet practices of water injection and overpumping, which lead to an early depletion of the reservoir at the expense of an extended production horizon.

Udmurt gains are expected to be quite minimal to 1985, perhaps growing by as little as 8,000 b/d over the course of the Eleventh Five Year Plan. Much of the oil in this province is heavy, requiring wide-scale steaming to reduce viscosity and improve the flow rate.[40]

Kazakhstan, having lost 100,000 b/d production since 1975 owing to reservoir depletions, is expected by Soviet officials to increase output by

Table 2-2
Non-Siberian Oil Basins, 1975 and 1981, Gains and Losses of
(*b/d*)

	1975	*1981*	*Change*
Kaliningrad	5,000	30,000	+ 25,000
Ukraine	256,000	135,000	− 121,000
North Caucasus	470,000	380,000	− 90,000
Georgia	56,000	60,000	+ 4,000
Azerbaijan	350,000	296,000	− 54,000
Turkemenia	310,000	180,000	− 130,000
Kuibyshev	690,000	462,000	− 228,000
Belorussia	160,000	50,000	− 110,000
Tataria	2.07[a]	1.5[a]	− 570,000
Udmurt Republic	70,000	172,000	+ 102,000
Komi ASSR	220,000	388,000	+ 168,000
Perm	450,000	278,000	− 172,000
Bashkiria	810,000	776,000	− 34,000
Orenburg	240,000	220,000	+ 20,000
Kazakhstan	480,000	380,000	− 100,000

Source: Adapted from "Oil Production Growth Rate Slowing Fast in Soviet Union," *Oil and Gas Journal*, November 30, 1981, p. 25.

[a] In mmbd.

1985 by as much as 120,000 b/d. Most of the increase is planned to come from the viscous oil reserves of the Caspian Sea's Mangyshlak Peninsula, in addition to offshore production in the southern Caspian Sea. Exploratory drilling has increased offshore, but more of the strikes will be natural gas and condensate rather than crude.[41] The Caspian accounts for all of the USSR's offshore production; preliminary Soviet data indicate good geological potential. Delays in the current Caspian offshore program, however, could continue to forestall the large output expected from this area by 1990.[42]

The Mangyshlak fields along the Caspian coast are characterized by a high paraffin content. This poses technical recovery problems requiring hot-water injection (150,000 cubic meters per day), with additional heating for pipeline transmission. Volga River water is now being pumped by pipeline into the Mangyshlak Peninsula, albeit at less than the required injection rate per day.[43]

There are two further caveats that must be borne in mind in regard to the Caspian depression. The Kazakhstan region as a whole is currently in decline, and onshore Caspian-area development is subject to a long-term drop in production. The probable cause of decline, as in other producing areas, was "brought on by an earlier decline in the recovery rate."[44]

The second problem foreseen for the Caspian region was set out by two petroleum geologists associated with the Argonne National laboratory.[45] Ulmishek and Harrison examined the petroleum potential of the Uzen field, a supergiant containing an estimated 7.5 billion barrels in place and whose production (which peaked in 1975) comprises 80 percent of Mangyshlak oil. The oil contains both high tar (as much as 21 percent) and high paraffin (as much as 28 percent) contents but a low sulfur content. The recovery efficiency was expected by Soviet authorities to equal 45 percent but is calculated by Ulmishek and Harrison to reach a maximum of 25 to 26 percent.[46] The initial water-cut expectation of 31 percent is instead calculated to approach 95 percent when the reservoir's cumulative output reaches 2 billion barrels.

The Uzen trend could be indicative of future Soviet production trends in basins of similar structure. The authors compare their results to the supergiant Samotlor field when they state that the exploitative pattern of:

> the Uzen field demonstrates the ineffectiveness of waterflooding in reservoirs having a complicated framework, especially for those reservoirs containing heavy and paraffinic oil. Intensification of production during the first stage of exploitation led to a rapid decline in output and a decrease in recovery efficiency.[47]

The results apply to those Soviet oil fields characterized by heavy and/or paraffinic oil content, in particular the following supergiants:

Russkoye in West Siberia, Arlan in the Urals-Volga, and Karazhanbas in the Buzachi Peninsula north of the Mangyshlak fields.[48] Since Russkoye, Arlan, and many smaller fields have undergone early intensive development and water flooding, the ability of large Uzen-type reservoirs to sustain long-term production stabilization is in serious doubt. The analogy with Samotlor holds grave implications for future production; Samotlor experienced "a significant rate of increase in water cut from irregularly distributed deltaic reservoir beds."[49]

Elsewhere, production prospects are not expected to make any significant inroads into national production gains through 1990. Sakhalin is currently producing 45,000 b/d with Japanese assistance; East Siberia has only had 1 percent of prospective oil land examined (about 35,000 square kilometers) but at this time appears to contain significantly more natural gas than oil.[50]

Similarly, in the offshore Arctic regions, the most easily exploitable sediments (close to shore) appear to exhibit too much maturation to contain abundant oil resources similar to West Siberia's supergiants. It is too early to tell, however, how successful future drilling will be. Farther offshore in the Kara Sea, East Siberian Seas, and Chuckchi Seas, vast hydrocarbon resources are assumed to exist, which could rival continental Soviet Eurasian reserves. Despite new Soviet equipment designed to drill at very deep depths (such as the Uralmash BU-15000 rig for drilling to 49,212 feet)[51] and several Finnish-built ice class drill ships for Arctic exploration,[52] the development time frame is too long for realization of any sizable gains by 1990.

Prospective personnel shortages worse than present shortfalls add to future Soviet production difficulties. In order to meet All-Union targets of 630 million tons (12.6 mmbd) by 1985, the number of drilling teams must be increased by one-third. The Ministry of Petroleum Industry will be hard pressed to achieve the drilling team increase because of the personnel shortages. Future Ministry efforts accordingly will focus on raising productivity.[53] Whether this can be accomplished is a matter of conjecture; above-plan drilling (as was achieved in 1981) does not guarantee large finds or productivity gains. Much of the future drilling in West Siberia and frontier areas will therefore be forced to achieve an increase in productivity at a time when most new discoveries are expected at depths below 9,000 feet. An infusion of Western technical aid probably would do little to alter production prospects by 1990.[54]

The oil-output trends to 1990 place Moscow in a difficult position. If the top party and government leaders involved in energy decision making choose to push their overextended giants and supergiants in West Siberia in an effort to increase production gradually, they run the risk of rapidly depleting their best fields by bringing on an accelerated decline in the reserves-to-production ratio. Depending on the size of the Soviet oil-reserve base—a difficult and uncertain estimate at best—production could fall rapidly by the latter 1980s should intensive development continue without sizable new additions to reserves.

If the Soviets pump at a decelerated pace, they may avoid the rapid fall-off in output but will then encounter difficulties satisfying domestic and bloc consumption. It is more likely that the leadership—in particular the party's energy overseers—will press ahead with past policies of overpumping and extensive water flooding. Most mature Soviet fields will not be able to sustain such treatment for much longer. The 1985 oil plan could be achieved but only at the expense of 1990 production. The period between 1986 and 1990 (the Twelfth Five Year Plan) would then prove particularly troublesome, as oil output falls and oil demand rises. Substitution of fuels therefore becomes a critical issue.

The CIA-DIA Dispute

Most Soviet energy studies to date have subjected the CIA analyses to close scrutiny. The DIA forecasts have not publicly undergone similar review. The apparent sentiment seems to be that the burden of proof lies with the pessimistic outlook, given the Soviet position as the world's leading oil producer.

The recent slowdown in oil-production gains should alter energy analysts' way of thinking about future levels of oil output. The energy-production trends in the USSR, particularly in oil but also in the other primary energy supplies (excepting natural gas), are downward sloping or negligibly rising throughout the 1980s. For this reason, close attention will be paid to the analysis offered by DIA in defense of its optimistic appraisal.

The CIA's previous positions have been set out on several occasions.[55] Pre-1981 CIA estimates assumed a relatively low reserve base (compared with other Western estimates) of about 33 billion barrels of proven oil. Peak production at Samotlor and other major producers would soon be reached; substitutes for oil could not be produced and brought to markets rapidly enough to affect the 1985 balance; oil exports for hard currency would correspondingly decline as bloc consumption needs rose.

Since the Warsaw Pact partners were projected to increase their hard-currency indebtedness, it appeared to the CIA that the group would not be able to afford oil imports at world prices. The prices charged by the Soviet Union were usually about 50 percent below OPEC levels, based on the CMEA's lagged moving five-year average of world oil prices. With little or no oil production of its own—Rumania's output peaked and was expected to decline—the bloc would suffer politically intolerable economic growth rates given the energy intensity of their economies. One option many in the

West presumed to have been debated in Moscow presented itself in particularly stark terms following the December 1979 invasion of Afghanistan:
a possible military move into the Persian Gulf region to secure supplies for
bloc utilization.

The CIA presented this Soviet option along with more-likely and less-
draconian measures open to the Soviet leadership: reallocation of resources
and policies at home, belt tightening in Eastern Europe, less-hostile over-
tures to Persian Gulf oil producers to obtain oil at concessional prices, and
perhaps covert action in the gulf region. I have suggested elsewhere that a
variety of low-intensity political moves (including coercive diplomatic
pressure and subversive operations), encouraged by a worsening bloc energy
and economic situation, would aim not to deny the West's oil flow but
rather to divert the minimally acceptable level for bloc disposition.[56]

The revised CIA estimate of 1981 expects 1985 production of 10 to 11
mmbd, as against earlier 1985 worst-case estimates of 8 to 10 mmbd.[57] The
change in estimates was caused by reported Soviet policy changes: increased
development drilling in West Siberia beyond previous expectations and
greater capital investment in both development and exploratory oil drilling.
No additions to reserves, however, have been indicated in the public record
as a result of the new investment and drilling.

The critical change in CIA thinking, then, relates to the increase in current (and planned) investment allocations, not a changed reserves-to-
production ratio. Indeed the CIA maintains that capital and labor costs
necessary to meet Soviet targets will be exceedingly high. A 1982 fuels-price
adjustment, the first such price rise since 1967, should contribute to conservation efforts but not enough to balance supply and demand in the mid-to-
late 1980s. Production in 1990 is still slated to fall to a low range of 7 to 9
mmbd. The shortfall cannot be countered because of the falling rate of
recovery in West Siberia, the lead-time lag associated with bringing new
reserves on-line, and the serious slippage of output in older producing
regions. Efficiency of production will not be improved by 1985 through importation of Western technology or internal Soviet efforts.

The DIA argument stands strongly in opposition to most of the CIA
views.[58] DIA places proven oil reserves at 80 billion to 85 billion barrels,
about 50 billion barrels more than the CIA estimates. They see Soviet oil
output slowly rising, leveling off in the late 1980s, and then rising again in
the 1990s. Oil-export earnings in 1985 should total $11.4 billion from the
sale to Western Europe of an estimated 34 million tons. Related DIA
forecasts include these prospects:

1. Slow economic growth, which will constrain demand.
2. A late 1980s coal-production upswing.

3. An increase in natural-gas output such that over 15 percent of production can be exported by the end of the decade.
4. Substitution of natural gas for oil where possible, with the shares of gas and nuclear rising steadily through the year 2000.

These are the general trends DIA foresees in primary Soviet energy production. There are a number of specific points DIA makes to support these trends; it is here that the dubious analyst must discover inconsistencies and analytical errors.

The Salym field will be an important producer after five to six years. PetroStudies of Sweden has estimated that the Salym field in West Siberia contains about 4.5 trillion barrels of recoverable reserves—approximately eight times more than *world* proven reserves. It is unclear whether DIA accepts this extraordinarily high reserve figure; their 1981 statement before the Joint Economic Committee refers to Salym's high-pressure oil and moderate and erratic well yields.[59] In the attached excerpts from testimony, however, the impression is given that while the "large find" at Salym (referred to by Senator William Proxmire as "colossal") was not quite the size PetroStudies claimed, it was "significant" and could be brought into production in "perhaps five to six years."[60] If the reported Salym find is an important factor in DIA's projection of Soviet ability to raise production in the 1990s, it is a mistaken assumption.

Salym is part of a "vast and complex bituminous shale formation present over a large part of Siberia."[61] The Bazhenov shale of which Salym is a part lies at a depth of at least 10,000 feet. The yields have been so low that the Soviets themselves disclaim any significant recoverable reserves with present recovery technology. Arthur A. Meyerhoff has similarly pointed out that "only a tiny fraction of the oil could be recovered and at an exorbitant cost."[62] The slow progress to date in U.S. oil-shale development featuring much greater technical expertise does not augur well for less-advanced Soviet attempts. The possibility of fracturing the shale by underground nuclear detonation, reportedly attempted in late 1979, appears to be a long shot at least for the present and near future. It is puzzling that the DIA did not make reference to Salym's shale composition.

Oil-Export revenues will be $11.4 billion in 1985. Most Soviet hard-currency sales of oil are purchased by Western Europe. In 1979, about 1.07 mmbd (or 85 percent) went to Western Europe of a total 1.2 to 1.3 (60 million to 65 million tons) mmbd sent to the free world.[63] The DIA disagrees slightly with this 1979 figure, citing an exports-to-Western-Europe figure of 1.16 mmbd (58.2 million tons). The plans announced in 1981 to reduce Soviet oil exports to Western Europe by 20 to 25 percent seem to be moving slower than expected and now appear to be a maximum level of exports in 1983-1985 should all other bloc-wide energy programs move forward. This would then leave, at most, 800,000 b/d (40 million tons), which at 1980 Soviet prices of $34.50/barrel would net Moscow approximately $10 billion per year.

The DIA foresees a drop in Western-Europe-bound exports in 1985 to a level of 680,000 b/d (34 million tons), which will bring in $11.4 billion in revenues. It believes that "the escalating price of crude oil" and the greater percentage of oil products that will then be available for export will combine to increase the current price by 28 percent. Thus the DIA sees the nominal price of Soviet oil in world markets as $44.16 per barrel in 1985. This would provide just under $11 billion per year from oil sales, not, as DIA states, $11.4 billion; however, additional calculations may have been factored in that would make up the $400 million discrepancy.

Assuming that noncommunist exports remain significantly in favor of Western Europe over other free-world buyers—though not at the 1979 level of 85 percent—a problem arises in the total exportable oil surplus projected by the DIA for 1985, 2.82 mmbd (141 million tons); 1.6 mmbd (80 million tons) are slated for Eastern Europe while 1.22 mmbd (61 millions tons) will be exported to the free world.[64] The DIA apparently believes that 27 million of the 61 million tons of noncommunist exports (44 percent) will be sold to developing countries for soft currencies, the implication being that the political benefits will outweigh the financial gain of $8.7 billion in hard-currency revenues (at the expected price of $44.16 per barrel). This does not seem probable in an era of tight financial constraints.

Two assumptions are built into the 1985 DIA scenario. The first grants an escalation of crude prices of 28 percent over 1980, resulting in a future nominal price of $44.16 per barrel. This is highly uncertain; buyers of Soviet crude attempted to negotiate price cuts in March 1982 of $4 to $5 per barrel (for cost, insurance, and freight prices of $29 to $30 per barrel). When British North Sea prices were slashed to $31 per barrel, "poorer quality Soviet crude would probably have to be priced under $30."[65] At least until the mid-1980s, the nominal price of oil in all probability will not rise much above current levels. There are, in fact, some indications that the Saudis would like to see the official OPEC price of $34 per barrel remain in effect until 1985-1986, when they believe the world economy will be ready for renewed nominal price escalation.

The other assumption relates to the future level of Soviet oil production and consumption. The DIA's production forecast of 12.5 mmbd (624 million tons) and its consumption forecast of 9.5 mmbd (475 million tons) appear too large and too small, respectively. It is unlikely that internal oil demand will stay below 10 mmbd (500 million tons), implying a downward revision in available export volumes. One reason among several can be attributed to the failure to reduce the energy-GNP ratio, especially for oil (and natural gas).[66] In late 1981, the Soviet Union cut oil exports to Eastern Europe (except Poland) by 10 percent, or 160,000 b/d (8 million tons).[67]

The 10-percent cut could well become institutionalized as an inducement to force oil-dependent Eastern European economies into more austere energy planning.

There is a strong probability, then, that Soviet exportable oil output will fall well below DIA projections, particularly in the mid-to-late 1980s, thus rendering the $11.4 billion earnings figure too high. Moscow must balance bloc considerations, its Third World strategy of oil diplomacy, and its hard-currency requirements with a declining additions-to-reserves base and a declining reserves-to-production ratio.

There is a further DIA comment that the USSR is capable of placing pressure "on world supplies and prices" while earning hard currency.[68] Rather than placing pressure on supplies and prices, however, it is more probable that Moscow will seek to take advantage of tight markets; it has not in the past and cannot in the future create tight markets. Soviet oil exports outside CMEA play too small a role in world exports and consumption to be able to influence price. In addition, it is a questionable assertion that the market-price trends by 1985 will be consistently upward as DIA asserts.

Oil output will stabilize and then increase. Despite increasing costs of production—such as for ancillary construction per oil-well borehole—the DIA projects West Siberian output of 7.7 to 7.9 mmbd (385 million to 395 million tons) as enabling the Eleventh Five Year Plan to be met.[69] The outlook past 1990 looks good to the DIA, regardless of the following problems:

1. The USSR "does not produce a number of high-technology items such as sophisticated computers for production control or digital processing of seismic data."
2. The USSR "has little experience in offshore operations and has relied on foreign sources for equipment and expertise."
3. Ministry of Petroleum Industry 1979 exploratory and appraisal drilling was concentrated in the European USSR, not West Siberia.
4. Since many of the largest fields have been tapped, the number of wells drilled must be increased because the average yield per well has significantly decreased.
5. In eastern Siberia, most discoveries to date "have been gas or condensate but the stratigraphy, tectonics, and maturation may occur at deeper depths in the Triassic and upper Paleozoic." In short, there may or may not be economically recoverable oil in East Siberia by the early 1990s.

The DIA, in a more-positive tone, assumes an increase in the number of available oil rigs during the Eleventh Five Year Plan, despite the declining trend witnessed in the Ninth and Tenth Five Year Plans. This will occur with the advent of new drilling organizations—eighty-three additional drilling brigades in West Siberia from 1981 to 1985—and an assumed 5 percent annual improvement in efficiency. Further, infrastructural requirements "are *probably* declining as the capacity of the transportation network is expanded"[71] (my emphasis). These developments should enable the West Siberian drilling targets to be met.

Much of the plan's development drilling, however, must occur at deeper depths than in previous years. It has been pointed out by the petroleum minister, N. Maltsev, "that drilling operations frequently remain behind schedule as a result of serious violations of 'technical discipline,' and that up to 7 percent of oil wells in several provinces are idle owing to excessive delays in the repair of equipment."[72]

New drilling organizations may be hard to come by as the personnel shortage worsens. The yearly increment of 2 million people joining the labor force in the Tenth Five Year Plan will be reduced to an average of 600,000 during the first four years of the Eleventh Five Year Plan and 400,000 in the last year. This may be compounded by ethnic and regional imbalances favoring non-Russian entrants.[73] The success of the flying-team method (into Siberia) may not be applicable in the latter 1980s when continued declines in production in the European provinces will require greater efforts at stemming the decline. When West Siberia begins registering shortfalls, skilled crews will be spread too thin to cover all the declines.

Finally, are infrastructural requirements declining as the USSR's transport network grows? This might be true if the pipeline system extended throughout the nation in a well-ordered and efficient fashion. As of 1980, however, over 40 percent of Soviet oil was still moved by rail, estimated at three times the expense of pipeline transportation.[74] The DIA itself has noted industrial shortages and shortfalls "attributed to lack of materials, including metals, fuel shortages, and transportation disruptions," especially rail.[75] *Pravda,* noted earlier for its support of oil and gas projects, reports that a yearly imported flow of some 200,000 tons of large-diameter pipe "will be sent by sea 'in future years' as overland transportation is *severely hampered* by *inadequate infrastructure*" (my emphasis).[76] Clearly, infrastructural growth will be necessary if an increase in efficiency and capacity is desired.

Efficiency of operations will be difficult to improve in areas where the permafrost extends down to 5,000 feet or more. Better equipment and new technology are necessary but present the oil-industry leadership with a dilemma: many of the advanced, sophisticated processes are "highly energy intensive" and will thus require greater inputs of primary energy in order to be effective.[77]

Table 2-3 illustrates the tenuous nature of the DIA projections; much is assumed about the Soviet ability to achieve what they say they are capable of achieving.

Table 2-3
West Siberia Oil Production

Date	Number of Producing Wells	Average Oil Production (metric tons)	Oil Production (million metric tons)
1970	1,200	71.6	31.5
1975	4,100	98.8	148
1978	8,000	86.9	254
1980	12,475	66.5	303
1985	35,886	29.4-30	385-395

Source: Major General Richard X. Larkin and Edward M. Collins, Defense Intelligence Agency, Statement before the Joint Economic Committee, Subcommittee on Economic Trade, Finance, and Security Economics, "Allocation of Resources in the Soviet Union and China—1981," July 8, 1981, p. 61.

As the number of producing wells increases and the average oil production per well decreases, the production of oil in West Siberia has grown by smaller increments: an increase of 116.5 million tons between 1970 and 1975, 155 million tons between 1975 and 1980, and 87 million tons projected growth between 1980 and 1985. Between 1975 and 1980, the average well yield decreased by 32.3 metric tons while West Siberian production grew by 155 million tons. In the period from 1980 to 1985, it is expected that new producing wells are to increase threefold, while average well yield decreases by an additional 36.5 metric tons and total regional production grows by 82 million to 92 million tons.

If the number of producing wells does not increase as rapidly as the DIA believes and if the average output per well falls to the range predicted (about 8 tons less than Gosplan has projected), it will be difficult to attain the regional increase. Given personnel, rig, and productivity constraints, it is doubtful that the Soviet oil output will be capable of expanding as productively as the DIA projects.

CMEA Oil Consumption

Oil consumption has been outstripping economic growth and growth in supply for some time. Soviet consumption of oil has grown at about 400,000 b/d (20 million tons) since the early 1970s, with 1980 consumption at about 9 mmbd (450 million tons). Eastern Europe consumed over 2.4 mmbd (120 million tons) in 1980, with average yearly increases slowing down but projected to pick up, despite minimal economic growth levels, to about 150,000 b/d (7.5 million tons).

The USSR provides over two-thirds of Eastern Europe's total oil consumption and 80 percent of Eastern Europe's oil imports. Excluding

Bulgaria and Rumania, the *Druzhba* (friendship) crude-oil pipeline from the Urals-Volga fields to Hungary, Czechoslovakia, Poland, and the GDR provides a sizable percentage of this oil flow. Non-Soviet bloc production, less than 400,000 b/d (20 million tons) and declining because of Rumania's fall in output, will present problems as the member-states experience diminishing returns in the planned substitution of gas for oil in industry and district heating, and as nuclear power meets with continual delays. With the expansion of the vehicle sector (for agricultural and private use), oil demand will continue its upward growth.[78]

Of the 9 mmbd (450 million tons) consumed in the USSR in 1980, approximately one-third each went to industry, transportation, and agriculture. Factoring in losses, nonenergy uses, storage tanks and stockfilling of new pipelines, and slowed growth in demand from conservation efforts, Tony Scanlan estimates a 1985 consumption range of between 9.7 and 10 mmbd (485 million to 500 million tons) and 10.8 mmbd (540 million tons).[79]

While Scanlan discounts the higher end of the range as improbable, it is interesting to note that industry—the largest consumer and waster of oil—is not expected to make significant conservation gains owing to the subordination of industrial conservation norms to the needs of production.[80] The rate of investment in the Eleventh Five Year Plan, however, is the lowest since World War II. Installation of expensive efficiency equipment on a massive scale is unlikely, and campaigns through the official media to conserve energy have been unsuccessful.[81] Gas substitution will run up against a practicable limit in two vital sectors: industry and district heating. As Leslie Dienes notes,

> In the concrete world of fluctuating heating schedules, of costly *in situ* equipment and, for gas, highly capital intensive storage and distribution facilities, the lumpiness of fixed capital and developmental lead times preclude the smooth and easy replacement of liquid products.[82]

Boiler requirements for oil may be expected to increase should delays in gas distribution, coal, and nuclear setback projected Soviet substitution among fuels. If oil production levels off at about current levels by 1985, the spread between supply and demand could be as little as 1.4 mmbd (70 million tons), enough for CMEA allies in Europe at present scaled-back deliveries with an assumption of falling East European oil demand, an unlikely prospect. There would then be no oil available for Western Europe and Japan, a situation that threatens 56 percent of Soviet hard-currency earnings at 1981 exports and prices. Unless natural-gas sales via the Siberian export line begin as scheduled with maximum capacities and no further delays, most of the current revenue from hard-currency oil sales will be lost.

Eastern Europe's oil demand, however, will not decline. Its oil needs comprise a small percentage of their energy mix compared with OECD economies, and the group is therefore greatly limited in its ability to conserve oil. Long-term programs aimed at greater coal and nuclear-power utilization and increased conservation will therefore prove of incremental value at best to 1990; the loss in efficiency stemming from coal conversions could bring in its wake a further lowering of industrial productivity.[83] Growth in oil demand is inevitable if economic growth above 1 or 2 percent is to be achieved. According to Scanlan, the end uses to which the growth in oil consumption are geared are rigidly fixed in applications incapable of (short-term) substitution (that is, the vehicle fleet, chemical feedstock factories).[84] For some positive level of growth to continue, oil demand will have to be satisfied at least at current levels and will probably increase, though at a slower pace than in the mid-1970s. However, Oleg Bogomolov of the USSR Institute of World Socialist Economics has stated that by 1990 half of Eastern Europe's oil supply would have to come from non-Soviet sources, assuming a continuation of current trends.[85] Since Soviet oil exports are slated to remain at 1980 levels (80 million tons) through 1985 with little prospect of additional growth to 1990, this would place his estimate of 1990 Eastern European demand at 3.2 mmbd (160 million tons).

The Soviet Union alone can fill this growing gap in Eastern Europe's supply. Oil from OPEC has doubled in price, and while the short-term world-price outlook to 1985 may be one of stability or decline, the longer term price trend to 1990 must be considered upward. The 20 percent of Eastern Europe's crude-oil imports supplied by OPEC will therefore remain stable or decline as the bloc loses its ability to gain loans from the West on a scale similar to that of the 1970s or simultaneously earn enough hard currency to pay for OPEC crude. With a larger proportion of CMEA labor and capital expended on joint projects with the USSR or on Soviet-bound exports—necessary to satisfy Moscow's growing energy and industrial needs—the bloc will have less capital for its non-Soviet oil-import needs for energy- and industrial-efficiency improvements and for reorientation of production toward Western markets.

A shortfall in Soviet oil deliveries—beyond the current 10-percent cutback—will result in still-lower growth for CMEA-Europe except for Rumania and Poland. These two member-states, however, will continue to experience economic difficulties despite their indigenous energy resources.

The lead time problem, made worse in the northern reaches by harsh climatic conditions and inefficient organizational procedures, plagues the USSR as it does the West. The DIA believes, as do the United Nations Economic Commission for Europe and PetroStudies of Sweden, that the 1980s oil supply and demand will not be unmanageable and that the 1990s hold the promise of still-greater oil and natural-resource recovery. If large volumes of economically recoverable oil exist in Siberia's vast outlying regions, it will take an inordinate amount of time and capital to explore, develop, and produce, with highly uncertain results. The top energy priority for the 1980s, however, may switch from oil to gas, rendering the maintenance of oil-stabilization and -growth programs suspect beyond the mid-1980s.

Notes

1. The 1977 reports were released in the following order: *Prospects for Soviet Oil Production; Prospects for Soviet Oil Production: A Supplemental Analysis; The International Energy Situation—The Outlook to 1985.*

2. The "Siberian pipeline" or "Siberian export pipeline" to Western Europe will be used throughout to denote the former Yamal or Yamburg project; the latter names referred to the original plan to develop the Yamburg natural-gas deposit on the Taz Peninsula (across from the Yamal Peninsula) and use this deposit as the source for West European deliveries. A decision was subsequently taken and announced in mid-1981 to delay the development of Yamburg and rely instead on the Urengoi deposit 150 miles south.

3. CIA, *Prospects for Soviet Oil Production: A Supplemental Analysis,* ER77-10425 (July 1977), p. 32; Jonathan P. Stern, "Western Forecasts of Soviet and East European Energy over the Next Two Decades (1980-2000)," U.S. Congress, Joint Economic Committee, *Energy in Soviet Policy* (June 11, 1981), p. 27 (hereafter referred to as JEC(1).) Stern lists reserves figures in billions of tons; for PetroStudies, the number is 20.5 billion tons. (Few analysts take the PetroStudies proved reserves figure seriously.) I have converted (and rounded) the figures given in tons by multiplying by 7.33 to arrive at a barrel-equivalent. One barrel equals 42 American gallons.

4. Stern, "Western Forecasts," p. 27. Soviet proven-reserves categories are listed as A + B + C1 in Soviet oil literature ranging from most easily accessible to most difficult. They are also referred to as industrial or commercial reserves. "Potential" or "probable" reserves range from categories C2 to D2, with D2 the least economically recoverable. Jeremy Russell, "Energy in the Soviet Union: Problems for Comecon?" *World Economy* (September 1981):312.

5. Theodore Shabad, "News Notes," *Soviet Geography* (April 1982):278.

6. Apart from Komi, those regions listed and the following areas—the North Caspian basin, the Pechora Basin, Kazakhstan, the Ukranian Carpathians, and the Western Urals belt—are cited by Danilo A. Rigassi, "Oil

and Gas in the USSR: There's a Lot of Both," *World Oil* (October 1981):213. Komi ASSR, often looked to as a major future producer, only . . . "accounted for 3.2 percent of USSR oil production after more than 9 years of development which is a slow start if it is to be an important producer." David H. Root and Lawrence J. Drew, "General Principles of the Petroleum Industry and Their Application to the USSR," JEC(1), p. 134.

7. B.A. Rahmer, "Soviet Union: Uncertain Prospects for Oil," *Petroleum Economist* (July 1981):294.

8. Robert E. Ebel, "Existing Sources of Crude Oil—Part 1, Soviet Union and China" (Presented at Platt's Oilgram/Conant and Associates Conference on World Trade in Hydrocarbons, September 21-22, 1981, p. 6.

9. Arthur A. Meyerhoff, "Energy Base of the Communist-Socialist Countries," *American Scientist* 69 (November-December 1981):627-628.

10. Joseph P. Riva, Jr., "Soviet Oil Prospects," Congressional Research Service, April 6, 1981, pp. 16-17, 11. Riva notes elsewhere that "new discoveries will have to be very large fields to be produced fast enough to impact the next decade, given the lead times in the vast frontier areas of the country." In "Soviet Petroleum Prospects: A Western Geologist's View," JEC(1), p. 125.

11. U.S. Congress, Office of Technology Assessment (OTA), *Technology and Soviet Energy Availability* (November 1981), pp. 37, 71-73, 74.

12. Statement of Major General Richard X. Larkin and Edward M. Collins, *Allocation of Resources in the Soviet Union and China—1981,* Defense Intelligence Agency (DIA) testimony before the Subcommittee on International Trade, Finance, and Security Economics, Joint Economic Committee, July 8, 1981, pp. 41-70. The reserves figures are given on p. 62.

13. "Oil Production Growth Rate Slowing Fast in Soviet Union," *Oil and Gas Journal,* November 30, 1981, p. 26.

14. Shabad, "News Notes"

15. The CIA has expected Samotlor, discovered in 1966, to peak for several years now. The *Oil and Gas Journal* wrote that "Samotlor is believed to have reached peak production of nearly 3.1 million b/d in 1980." Samotlor, estimated to contain 2 billion tons of oil, passed the first-billion-ton mark on July 27, 1981. "USSR's Biggest Oil Field Passes Milestone," *Oil and Gas Journal,* August 31, 1981, p. 30. Rigassi, "Oil and Gas in the USSR," in an optimistic appraisal of the Soviet energy future, claims that Samotlor has reached peak capacity.

16. Demonstrated reserves refer to "proved and indicated additional" reserves; inferred reserves refer to "anticipated field growth in existing fields." Charles D. Masters, "Assessment of Conventionally Recoverable Petroleum Resources of the West Siberian Basin and Kara Sea Basin,

U.S.S.R.," U.S. Department of the Interior Geological Survey, Open—File Report 81-1147 (1981), pp. 2, 6. Hereafter USGS-1.

17. Riva, "Soviet Oil Prospects," p. 11.

18. Two of the more-notable optimists who have pointed to (among other factors) the relative lack of exploration and the vastness of Soviet potential are Marshall Goldman, *The Enigma of Soviet Petroleum: Half-Empty or Half-Full?* (London: George Allen & Unwin, 1980), and Jonathan P. Stern, *Soviet Natural Gas Development to 1990: Implications for the CMEA and the West* (Lexington, Mass.: Lexington Books, D.C. Heath and Company, 1980).

19. Masters, USGS-1, p. 7.

20. Ibid.

21. The petroleum potential of that particular age rock worsens as one moves west in Tyumen Oblast.

22. Root and Drew, "General Principles," p. 137. The authors conclude that "the maintenance of level oil production requires the application of conservationalist policies and such application is not evident in the production histories of four World class giants (Samotlor, Arlan, Tuymazy, Romashkino) or in their four most productive areas (North Caucasus, Central Asia and Kazakhstan, Volga-Urals, West Siberia)" (p. 138).

23. The previous two paragraphs closely follow the argument presented in Riva, "Soviet Oil Prospects," pp. 20-22.

24. Rahmer, "Soviet Union," p. 294; DIA, *Allocation of Resources,* p. 60.

25. DIA, *Allocation of Resources,* p. 51.

26. Theodore Shabad, "News Notes," *Soviet Geography* (April 1981): 274.

27. "Communist Bloc Barely Scored Oil Flow Increase in 1981," *Oil and Gas Journal,* March 8, 1982, p. 102; DIA, *Allocation of Resources,* p. 57. The DIA figures are given in meters; I have converted to feet and rounded.

28. "Oil Production Growth Rate Slowing Fast," p. 24. The report further states that 90 percent of all oil-industry capital outlays go toward maintaining current production, which is not encouraging for exploratory drilling. For every 1 ton increase in All-Union output, production of 8 tons in West Siberia was necessary during the Tenth Five Year Plan. It is plausible that this ratio will increase during the Eleventh and Twelfth Five Year Plans (1981-1985 and 1986-1990, respectively).

29. Ibid., p. 26.

30. "Eastern Europe: Policies Are Changing," *World Oil,* August 15, 1981, p. 206.

31. Ronda Bresnick and John P. Hardt, "Soviet Energy Debate and Scenarios for Coping with Their Energy Problems," JEC(1), pp. 162-163.

32. A. Aleksandrov, "Prospects for Power Engineering," *Izvestia,* February 21, 1981, p. 2, translated in *Current Digest of the Soviet Press* as "Surveying the USSR's Energy Future," April 1, 1981, p. 3.

33. Y. Permiken, "In Northern Versions," *Pravda,* November 14, 1980, p. 2, translated in "Tyumen Needs Special Oil, Gas Machinery," *Current Digest of the Soviet Press,* December 17, 1980, p. 11.

34. A. Kleva, L. Levitsky, Yu. Perepletkin, and G. Shipitko, "Winter Makes Stern Demands," *Izvestia,* September 27, 1980, p. 2, translated in "The Economy," *Current Digest of the Soviet Press,* October 29, 1980, pp. 17-18.

35. The 5 million ton per year figure is a Soviet expectation. Tony Scanlan, "Outlook for Soviet Oil" (Paper presented at Conference on Oil and Money in the Eighties: New Outlooks, London, September 1981), p. 25. Additionally, Scanlan points out that Soviet oil production could fall by 2 mmbd by 1990 owing to western USSR regional declines and the projected failure of Samotlor, now one-quarter of All-Union output, to produce at peak levels.

36. Charles D. Masters and James A. Peterson, "Assessment of Conventionally Recoverable Petroleum Reserves of the Volga-Urals Basin, U.S.S.R.," U.S. Department of the Interior Geological Survey, Open-File Report 81-1027 (1981), pp. 6-7.

37. Shabad, "Geographical Distribution of Soviet Oil Production."

38. Riva, "Soviet Petroleum Prospects," pp. 123, 121.

39. A. Skrypnik, "The Timan Ridge," *Pravda,* September 1, 1980, p. 2, translated in "Timan-Pechora Area Yields Oil, Gas, Coal," *Current Digest of the Soviet Press,* October 1, 1980, pp. 9-10.

40. "Oil Production Growth Rate Slowing Fast," p. 27.

41. "Caspian Sea to Remain Soviets' Prime Exploration Target through This Decade," *Oil and Gas Journal,* October 12, 1981, p. 166. OTA, *Technology,* p. 2, notes that "the entire Caspian region is not expected to resume a major producing role."

42. "Eastern Europe," p. 211.

43. Theodore Shabad, "Kazakhstan Desert Oilfield Gets Volga Water through Pipeline," *Soviet Geography* (June 1981):393-395.

44. Root and Drew, "General Principles," p. 134.

45. G. Ulmishek and W. Harrison, Argonne National Laboratory, "Uzen Development Gives New Insight into Projecting Future Soviet Oil Output," *Oil and Gas Journal,* August 24, 1981, pp. 148-154. The discussion of Uzen follows the Ulmishek and Harrison article.

46. This figure is identical with a CIA recovery figure of 26 percent for West Siberia given the necessary gas-lift equipment. CIA, *Prospects,* p. 32.

"Historically, growth of water-cut has been accompanied by a decreasing average yield per well" Ulmishek and Harrison, "Uzen Development," p. 154.

47. Ulmishek and Harrison, "Uzen Development," p. 154.

48. Ibid., p. 148.

49. Ibid., p. 154.

50. "Soviet Union: Prospective Oil Provinces," *Petroleum Economist,* (May 1981):216.

51. "Soviets to Build More Big Rigs in Push for Superdeep Drilling," *Oil and Gas Journal,* December 7, 1981, p. 80. Twelve BU-15000s are planned for. At the rate the Soviets are drilling in the Kola Peninsula test hole, the 49,000-foot depth will be reached by late 1987.

52. "Soviet Union Starts Its First Drilling Project in Arctic Waters," *Oil and Gas Journal,* February 22, 1982, pp. 39-42. The Kara Sea in the western Arctic looks best for hydrocarbon potential, but conditions are hostile and natural gas seems to predominate. An OTA study published in October 1980 concludes that "it is unlikely that the offshore Arctic areas will be developed this century. The conditions in these areas are such that the technology for development does not currently exist even in the West." *World Petroleum Availability 1980-2000: A Technical Memorandum,* pp. 66-67.

53. "Soviet Union: Drilling Performances to Be Improved," *Petroleum Economist* (December 1981):539.

54. Ronda Bresnick and John P. Hardt, "Soviet Economic Policy toward West Europe," JEC(1), p. 87: "Without a substantial increase in domestic investment for building an effective infrastructure, the use of Western technology, especially in Siberian energy projects, will likely fall far short of its potential effectiveness."

55. See note 1 for previous CIA forecasts. Other CIA oil analyses include *The World Oil Market in the Years Ahead,* ER79-10327U (August 1979); *The Soviet Economy in 1978-79 and Prospects for 1980,* ER80-10328 (June 1980); Admiral Stansfield Turner, "The Geopolitics of Oil," Senate Energy and Natural Resources Committee testimony, April 1980.

56. Jonathan B. Stein, "Soviet Energy: Current Problems and Future Options," *Energy Policy* (December 1981):301-315. An additional benefit would accrue to Moscow in the form of higher oil prices flowing from a major crisis in the Persian Gulf. This windfall can only be realized while the Soviets are still exporting a substantial amount of oil for hard currency.

57. Joseph A. Licari, "Linkages between Soviet Energy and Growth Prospects for the 1980's," in *CMEA: Energy 1980-1990* (Brussels: NATO Economics Directorate, April 8-10, 1981); Steve Mufson, "CIA Alters Its Soviet Oil Forecast," *Wall Street Journal,* May 18, 1981, p. 31; "CIA

Estimate of Soviet Oil Production Is Expected to Upgrade Moscow's Ability," *Energy Users Report,* May 14, 1981, pp. 809-812.

58. The reference to the DIA forecast follows the DIA testimony in statement of Larkin and Collins, *Allocation of Resources;* see also James Naughtie, "DIA Study Boosts Estimate of Worth of Soviet Energy Reserves," *Washington Post,* September 3, 1981, p. 1; Bernard Gwertzman, "Soviet Is Able to Raise Production of Oil and Gas, U.S. Agency Says," *New York Times,* September 3, 1981, p. 1.

59. DIA, *Allocation of Resources,* p. 54.

60. DIA, "Excerpts from Testimony," in ibid., pp. 125-126. The rise in production expected by the DIA in the 1990s appears in part to be based on anticipated success in developing Salym. See Naughtie, "DIA Study."

61. Riva, "Soviet Oil Prospects," p. 22.

62. For the Soviet disclaimer, see "Soviets Deny Swedish Report on Big Reserves in Oil Field," *Washington Post,* March 16, 1981, p. A15; for Meyerhoff's comment, see Douglas Martin, "Report of Soviet Oil Find Ridiculed in U.S.," *New York Times,* December 6, 1980, p. 30. James W. Clarke and Jack Rachlin of the USGS are paraphrased as saying that the shale formation in question may contain about 15 trillion barrels, but only a "tiny" portion can be produced "since the rock is not extensively fractured, it remains in the rock rather than accumulating in pools from which it can be pumped." John M. Berry, "False Report of Huge Soviet Oil Find Briefly Unsettles Financial Markets," *Washington Post,* December 6, 1980, p. A26. Scanlan, "Outlook," p. 25, notes similar problems at Salym.

63. CIA, "International Energy Statistical Review," January 26, 1982, p. 25. *Petroleum Intelligence Weekly,* June 1, 1982, put 1980 West European imports of Soviet oil at 1.06 mmbd (53 million tons), p. 9, and in 1981 OECD imports of Soviet oil totaled 1.03 mmbd (51.4 million tons, of which 28.8 million were crude and 22.6 million were products). International Energy Agency, *World Energy Outlook,* Paris: OECD, 1982, p. 176.

64. DIA, *Allocation of Resources,* p. 44.

65. *Petroleum Intelligence Weekly,* March 15, 1982, p. 12.

66. Edward A. Hewett, CSIS Seminar on Soviet Energy Prospects. According to Hewett, the Soviet energy-to-GNP ratio is about 1.3; for oil-GNP the ratio is between 1.5 and 2.0, and for natural-gas-GNP the ratio is about 2.0. Oil consumption in 1981 rose twice as fast as GNP.

67. Anthony Robinson, "The Soviet Economy: Why Something Has to Give," *Financial Times,* February 5, 1982.

68. DIA, *Allocation of Resources,* p. 42.

69. Ibid., pp. 68-69.

70. Ibid., pp. 52, 53, 61, 64.

71. Ibid., pp. 56, 58, 59.

72. As reported in "News in Brief," *Petroleum Economist* (August 1981):360.

73. DIA, *Allocation of Resources,* p. 8. Population-growth rates are expected to decrease from 2.2 percent per year to 0.5 percent per year during the 1980s. R.T. Maddock, "Oil and Economic Growth in the Soviet Union," *Three Banks Review* (March 1980):30.

74. Maddock, "Oil and Economic Growth," p. 34.

75. DIA, *Allocation of Resources,* p. 6.

76. As reported in "News in Brief," *Petroleum Economist* (March 1981):124.

77. Maddock, "Oil and Economic Growth," p. 33.

78. Scanlan, "Outlook," pp. 12-14.

79. Ibid., pp. 14-15.

80. Ibid., p. 11.

81. John P. Hardt, "Soviet and East European Energy Policy: Security Implications" (paper presented to Conference on the Future of Nuclear Power in the Federal Republic of Germany, December 1981), p. 19. Hardt also notes (p. 20), "Transportation of energy supplies may also be a source of bottlenecks . . . the rail transport system is overloaded and subject to frequent interruptions.

82. Leslie Dienes, "Energy Conservation in the USSR," in JEC(1), p. 106. Stemming energy demand through curbing allocation in major consuming sectors "is far less likely to be successful given the nature of the planning process, the influence of these branches and the vested interest of the leadership." Bureaucratic, structural, and geographic barriers "will force the continued, large scale burning of hydrocarbons, especially oil, in economically sub-optimal uses." Ibid., p. 102.

83. Robin A. Watson, "The Linkage between Energy and Growth Prospects in Eastern Europe," in U.S. Congress, Joint Economic Committee, *East European Economic Assessment; Part 2—Regional Assessments,* July 10, 1981, p. 504.

84. Scanlan, "Outlook," p. 21.

85. Thane Gustafson, "Energy and the Soviet Bloc," *International Security* (Winter 1981-1982):49.

3

CMEA in the 1980s

The CMEA faces a difficult decade. A growing labor and materials short-age, increasing prices for scarce fuels, and an unparalleled hard-currency in-debtedness leave the organization's future economic prospects in danger of further stagnation. Regime stability in Eastern Europe derives in large part from real increases in economic growth, which in turn often grant political legitimacy to the uppermost circles of national leadership. Poland is but the most-striking example of the relationship between ruling elites and eco-nomic performance.

An examination of Soviet and East European fuels trade provides the necessary context in which to assess the political and strategic implications of Soviet-bloc energy development and utilization. Economic success or failure in Eastern Europe and the USSR will become more important in the 1980s as determinants of Soviet foreign-policy behavior, and as such CMEA prospects must be discussed and debated in the West.

Alternatives to Oil

For certain uses, such as mobility fuels, there is no economical alternative to oil. In stationary applications or for electricity generation, other fuels may be more cost effective or thermally efficient. The CMEA's supply and de-mand for natural gas, coal, nuclear power, and renewable fuels will be ad-dressed in this section.

Natural Gas

Natural gas has assumed tremendous importance in Soviet energy and economic planning. It could well become the Soviet bloc hydrocarbon of the future as both party and government leaders agree that its export-earning potential and substitutability in many bloc applications make its timely development imperative. The completion of the internal gas-pipeline network, including the export line to Western Europe, should greatly facilitate Soviet natural-gas distribution, a principal bottleneck in the gas sector.

Proven Soviet gas reserves are abundant. Six fields in northwest Siberia contain over 1 trillion cubic meters (tcm) each, and total gas reserves are placed at 28 tcm, about 40 percent of world reserves.[1] Production increased by 9 percent each year during the Tenth Five Year Plan, slowing somewhat by 1980-1981 but still reaching 465 bcm in 1981. East European gas production is not extensive, with the exception of Rumania. About 52 percent of East Europe's gas supply is imported from the USSR. Rumania's gas output peaked in 1976, however, and Rumania began to import some Soviet gas in 1979. Figure 3-1 displays the major gas deposits and connecting pipelines (including planned projects).

The Orenburg natural-gas complex some 200 miles east of the Volga River, and the connecting 1,700-mile Soyuz pipeline to Eastern Europe, is the most successful CMEA project to date. All of CMEA-Europe participated in financing the construction of the project, with repayment in the form of yearly gas imports of 2.8 bcm (with the exception of Rumania, which will receive 1.5 bcm) for twenty years starting from 1979. Throughput capacity of the Soyuz pipeline is 28 bcm. In 1980, natural gas from Orenburg constituted 17 percent of Eastern Europe's apparent gas consumption.[2]

The Soviet gas plan becomes very significant given the likelihood of falling oil production. Gosplan has announced a revised 1985 target of 630 bcm, narrowing the range on the high side of the initial goal of 600 to 640 bcm. Despite the past and present success of the natural-gas industry, I do not believe that 1985 and 1990 production targets are realistic. Several prominent Western energy analysts also are skeptical of Soviet projections.

Edward Hewett of the Brookings Institution cites equipment and organization as major constraints in meeting the ambitious Eleventh Five Year Plan. The six pipelines intended for domestic consumption and export will have to be built "at a pace more than twice that of previous years;" construction and labor problems at the northern gas deposits and along designated transport routes hinder infrastructural support and add to the problems of equipment reliability and untimely delivery. Hewett projects 1985 natural-gas output at 599 bcm (58 billion cubic feet per day) with total exports of 100 bcm (9.67 billion cubic feet per day).[3] Apparent consumption—"gross production minus a net trade figure"—would then be 499 bcm, a figure lower than other Western-projected consumption levels.[4]

Jonathan P. Stern, citing a tremendous reserve and resource base and the Soviet penchant for "gigantism in economic organization," foresees a 1985 total output of 610 bcm. With gas consumption in the Soviet bloc increasing much faster than GNP and growing at about 6 percent per year through 1985 within the Soviet Union, consumption of gas would be 520 bcm, leaving 90 bcm for export to Western and Eastern Europe.[5]

A yearly 6 percent growth rate in Soviet gas consumption may be too small, however. A growth rate of 7 percent per year may be more accurate,

Source: Office of Technology Assessment (OTA), from *Technology and Soviet Energy Availability*, Washington, D.C., November 1981, p. 61.

Figure 3-1. Major Gas Pipelines, USSR

according to James Ellis of the Economics Directorate of the North Atlantic Treaty Organization (NATO).[6] If this comes to pass, then there will be correspondingly less gas for export. With declining oil earnings, Eastern Europe would not then realize increased gas shipments. The bulk of the projected Soviet surplus—at least 60 to 65 bcm from existing contracts and additions from the Siberian export project—would be sold for hard-currency to Western Europe.

Still others believe that USSR gas consumption will grow faster than production. Hannigan and McMillan believe the gas plan too optimistic and see Soviet oil declines and gas-for-oil substitution requiring an outpacing of gas production by gas consumption. The loss of about 10 bcm of annual Iranian imports and the expanded commitments taken on as a result of the Siberian export plans indicate a drop in the share (from 7 percent to 5 percent) of Soviet gas exports to Eastern Europe over 1980 levels, but not in the total volume delivered: 31.5 bcm.[7]

In the Hannigan-McMillan scenario, there will probably not be as much exportable gas in 1985 as planned for in 1981. If Stern's consumption figure is too conservative, then Moscow will be placed in a position analogous to its oil decisions: which commitments to keep and which to break.

Coal

In the 1960s and early 1970s, a shift in Eastern European consumption solidified away from coal and toward oil and natural gas. These were more-efficient and cleaner fuels and facilitated the development of chemical industries and the automotive-transport sector.[8]

Use of coal, however, remained predominant. Poland, the GDR, and Czechoslovakia use oil for only 20 percent of their consumption. Hungary, Rumania, and Bulgaria use more oil in their energy mix (about 35 percent), but this too is significantly less than OECD consumes. Further, except for Rumania, flexibility is lacking. Eighty percent of electricity capacity in Bulgaria and the GDR is provided by solid fuels, mostly hard coal and lignite; the percentage is over 90 percent in Poland and Czechoslovakia, about 70 percent for Hungary, and more than 50 percent in Rumania.[9]

This presents problems for at least two reasons. Investment in Polish, GDR, and Czech coal projects has become "increasingly unproductive," as the quality and calorific content on a Btu basis decreases and investment elsewhere realizes higher rates of return.[10] The same applies to the Soviet coal industry, which faces a "much more unfavorable" investment-to-production ratio than do oil or gas.[11] Costs rise precipitously as mine depletion worsens, deeper ores must be extracted and distances from major consuming centers grow (see figure 3-2). For much of Eastern Europe, therefore,

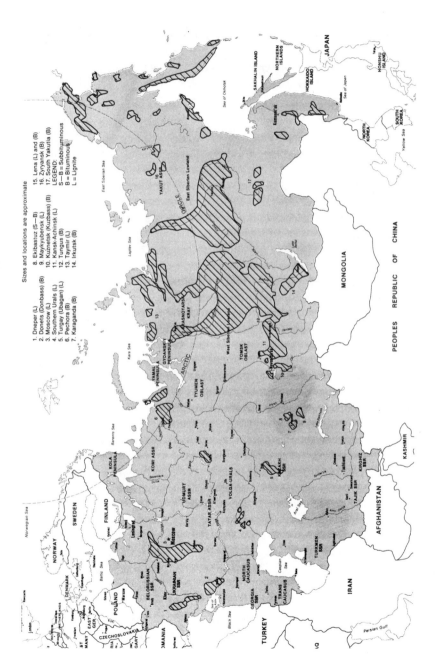

Source: Office of Technology Assessment (OTA), from *Technology and Soviet Energy Availability*, Washington, D.C., November 1981, p. 85.

Figure 3-2. Soviet Coal Basins

reliance on coal imports or oil and gas substitutes from the USSR becomes more economically attractive.

The second problem relates to substitution. With financial resources in Eastern Europe projected to be even tighter than at present, the investment capital necessary for mass conversions out of coal may not be available. The time frame may be off as well:

> For furnaces and boilers, where fuel substitution is easier and more effective, special equipment has to be added to burn a different fuel. The time required for this conversion, accounting for bottlenecks in equipment used for this purpose, is considerable.[12]

Additionally, the cost of additional Soviet oil and gas is rising (Eastern Europe pays world prices for above-quota shipments); thus, the bloc will not have the luxury of choosing one economical alternative over another. Both boiler conversions and added gas or oil usage will be expensive.

Soviet coal production fell 12 million tons in 1981 to 704 million tons, despite an estimated reserve base of 240 billion tons.[13] Polish coal output in 1981 fell victim to the nation's political upheaval, declining from 193 million tons in 1980 to 163 million tons in 1981. Polish coal exports were cut in half, with 8 million tons each shipped to CMEA and the West (see table 3-1). Exports of Soviet coal fell by 2 million tons in 1981 to 3 million tons, with 1.5 million tons each to Western Europe and Japan.[14] The GDR and Czechoslovakia each produce over 100 million tons of coal per year, but the overwhelming majority is lignite, a low-grade coal with a tendency to self-ignite, thus precluding long-distance transport.[15]

Lignite and brown coal are "inferior fuels not only in their calorific content but in their handling properties and, above all, in their expense." Except for Poland, the share of lignite and brown coal in Eastern Europe's

Table 3-1
Trends in Polish Coal Exports
(millions of tons)

	1979	1980	1981
Total exports	41	31	16
To West	26.4	17	8
Steam coal	18.7	11	6
Metallurgical coal	7.7	6	2
To CMEA	15	14	8
Steam coal	14.3	13.5	7.5
Metallurgical coal	0.7	0.5	0.5

Source: Adapted from "World Status: Coal Trade," chart on Poland's declining coal exports, *Energy Economist* (February 1982):13.

coal mix is increasing. Coal expenditures occupy a significant share of bloc energy budgets. In 1977, coal accounted for over 70 percent of energy spending in Poland and the GDR and over 60 percent for Czechoslovakia.[16] This does not factor in the high degree of dependence on coal production by certain key sectors: electricity generation or steel output.

These shares are difficult to reduce because of the energy intensiveness of most Soviet bloc economies. Compared to the OECD, CMEA nations require 70 to 80 percent more energy to produce one unit of national income.[17] In large part, the problem can be traced to the Soviet model of economic development: the focus is on gross output, not inputs, while heavy industries receive the bulk of capital investment. Heavy industries consume the lion's share of primary-energy inputs, but Eastern Europe cannot sustain these industries from its domestic resource base as can the Soviet Union.[18]

Personnel shortfalls in Soviet coal mines will pose additional hardships as coal-worker productivity continues to fall. In the Donetsk coal basin in the Soviet Ukraine, union crimes have been chronicled by the Soviet press, and worker dissatisfaction has impeded mining productivity.[19] Donetsk, though registering small yearly declines, is the most-productive coal basin, contributing just under 200 million tons of a 1981 total of 704 million tons.[20]

The poor-quality lignites of the Kansk-Achinsk Basin in southern Siberia and the subbituminous coal of the Ekibastuz Basin in Khazakhstan are planned for use either in coal liquefaction to produce liquid fuels or in mine-site long-distance, ultrahigh voltage (UHV) transmission of electricity to the European USSR. The goal of a series of interlocking electricity grids is bolstered by Soviet investment in transmission research, but "the task of bringing electricity from the East to the European part of the country requires the construction and operation of UHV lines at unprecedented voltages."[21] Further, with the proportion of strip-mining gaining on deep mining, much will depend on the reliability of Soviet machine-building industry. The equipment necessary for successful strip-mining—large-capacity power shovels, dragline excavators, large-capacity stripping and loading equipment, and heavy off-the-road trucks—lags behind that needed to fulfill the ambitious strip-mine plans decreed for 1990.[22]

With Polish and Soviet coal exports to CMEA in danger of further slippage as a result of inadequate production, Eastern Europe may be forced to rely more on nuclear power or conservation if costly oil or gas switching proves too expensive. Nuclear power is now being promoted as the best alternative to long-term reliance on fossil fuels for stationary purposes.

Nuclear Power

The Soviet-bloc nations are singularly committed to the widescale expansion of nuclear power. Eastern Europe in particular, lacking any sizable hydrocarbon resource base, has set its hopes on the rapid fulfillment of Soviet and indigenous nuclear-electricity programs. Eastern Europe currently has approximately 3,500 megawatts (MW) of installed capacity, short of earlier plans by 2,500 MW. The USSR, with thirty-two operative reactors, has 13,000 MW of installed nuclear capacity, short by about one-third the capacity planned in 1971.[23]

The plans to 1990 can only be characterized as unrealistic. For all of CMEA-Europe, the target was 150,000 MW of installed capacity, 37,000 MW of which was intended for Eastern Europe.[24] This projection has since been scaled back to about 120,000 MW. By 1990, then, over 100,000 MW are scheduled to be installed at great cost, a staggering level of growth. In addition to the 37,000 MW planned to meet East European demand, still more power is to come from two jointly planned stations on Soviet territory: the 4,000 MW Khmelnitskii nuclear reactor in the western Ukraine, and a 750 kilovolt line from Khmel to Rzeszow, Poland. Half of the electricity produced from these projects will be exported to Poland, Hungary, and Czechoslovakia.[25] Nuclear-power growth is planned to provide 25 percent of Eastern Europe's electricity consumption by 1990; this averaged figure is lower for Poland and Rumania but higher in the GDR (30 percent) and Bulgaria (50 percent).[26]

Specialization among bloc members allows each country to contribute certain reactor components for the final product, while promoting economic and political integration. When production is not running smoothly, though, and bottlenecks in one country affect output and consumption in the others, regional integration plans are upset. The Soviet Union and Czechoslovakia are primarily responsible for end-use reactor production. Each has experienced mounting problems in their ambitious programs, and serious economic problems in the remaining bloc countries will compound delays.

The Skoda works in Czechoslovakia is scheduled to turn out eight VVER-440 units (Soviet-style reactors that produce 440 MW each of electricity) for domestic use and a similar number for export to CMEA-Europe during the 1980s. Construction of the first 1,000 MW reactor in Czechoslovakia is planned for the second half of the decade. Before the current Five Year Plan began, Czech planners announced that present capacity of 880 MW would be expanded to over 10,000 MW by 1990, a target subsequently scaled back in 1981 to a 1990 goal of 7,520 MW.[27]

The lower target may not be met either. The nuclear-power station at Joslovske Bohunice was expected to have twice its current capacity by 1985, and four 440 MW units were scheduled to be built at Dukovany. Both stations are well behind the revised schedule. Steel shipments are lagging, skilled workers are in short supply (especially those from Poland), and poor management and rationalization of effort are lacking.[28]

In the GDR, nuclear-electricity targets were curtailed as domestically produced lignites were planned to pick up the slack. Equipment delays and cost overruns of about 60 percent plague the Hungarian program. Unrest in Poland has hurt both the Czech and the Soviet efforts. The Poles are responsible for supplying materials to the Khmelnitskii joint venture (for the export of electricity from Soviet soil), for joint construction of Soviet nuclear stations at Smolensk and Kursk, and for construction of a critical switching station at Rzeszow in Poland, which would channel Soviet-supplied electricity from Poland to Hungary, the GDR, and Czechoslovakia.[29] Labor problems in Poland may not be capable of early resolution, despite claims from martial-law authorities that military rule would improve productivity and strengthen the economy.

At a July 1981 Soviet Central Committee conference on the Eleventh Five Year Plan, Soviet nuclear-power goals were elucidated in greater detail. Generating capacity is expected to triple, as is electricity generation, from 73 billion kilowatt-hours (kWh) to 220 billion to 225 billion kWh. If that goal is realized, nuclear power in 1985 would represent 11 percent of installed capacity and 14 percent of electricity generation, up from 4.7 percent and 5.6 percent, respectively.[30] That would leave an additional 50,000 MW of planned capacity to be installed during the Twelfth Five Year Plan (1986-1990), a herculean task given present conditions and trends. Ten thousand MW of new capacity is expected to be installed each year by the end of the 1980s; three-quarters of the new capacity will be built in the European USSR, where 80 percent of the population lives.[31]

Construction of future nuclear-power stations increasingly will turn on the success of Attomash, an assembly complex in Volgodonsk designed to build eight reactor vessels per year at 1,000 MW capacity cach. Construction of a series of 1,600 MW breeder reactors is also planned. But the complex is several years behind schedule and is not now estimated to reach full capacity until 1990. Costs are extremely high, and intermediate industries have been lax in supplying the necessary equipment, notably steel, while personnel morale and productivity are quite low. Power-plant construction at other sites suffer from similar problems.[32]

Safety concerns, although not comparable to those in the West, have begun to enter into Soviet discussions and designs of nuclear reactors. After the accident at Three Mile Island in the United States, containment vessels were incorporated into standard Soviet designs. The USSR enforces strict export requirements in reactor sales and enrichment services abroad, in part because of an active concern with nonproliferation but also from a desire to placate European fears of nuclear-associated environmental damage. The past problems the Soviets have experienced with their nuclear-power program—in particular the Ural Mountains waste-storage explosion in 1958 and the Soviet-built reactor fatalities in Czechoslovakia in 1976—have received much publicity in the West.[33] If reactor sales for hard-currency are to be increased, then greater concern with safety features will probably delay the nuclear effort.

Soviet reactor supplies to CMEA-Europe is intended to supplement skilled-personnel cooperation and technical assistance to those countries' programs. As Thane Gustafson of Rand has noted, "This will come at a time when the Soviet Union is mounting a crash nuclear power program of its own." The competition between Eastern Europe and the Soviet Union for scarce high-performance materials and skilled labor could create tensions at a time when peak-coverage demand will outpace supply.[34]

Finally, some of the current problems plaguing the nuclear industry were discussed in *Pravda* by P. Neporozhny, the Soviet minister of power and electrification. Special alloy steels are in short supply, threatening a delay of the construction of new nuclear-power plants; metallurgy and electrometallurgy, responsible for production of the special alloys, will in turn be held up by the shortage of electrical-power supply. Inefficient planning at Attomash and the lag in materials deliveries are two universal problems that need to be overcome.[35]

The rapid expansion of nuclear power is closely linked with the Soviet objective of creating an All-Union Unified Power System (UPS), which would join eleven existing joint-power systems in the USSR and eventually the East European electrical grid. Sophisticated minicomputers and data-transmission and data-control equipment appear to be the major constraints. The European-USSR UPS (which comprises eight of the eleven joint systems and includes some non-European regions) is, however, a precariously connected network controlled "from a single, underequipped dispatching office in Moscow."[36] Assuming that there will be sufficient fuels availability for conversion to the necessary quantities of electrical power planned for in 1985 and 1990, a further problem arises in the engineering for long-distance UHV transmission, "a relatively new field" for the USSR, "which, at least initially, will entail high investment and operating costs."[37] If there is insufficient fuels availability, particularly from unmet coal targets and postponement of boiler conversions from oil to gas, then delays in the nuclear-power program will add to the dim prospects for an early and efficient realization of the UPS.

Alternative Fuels Industries

The development of alternative-fuels industries increasingly is receiving more attention. The late President Leonid Brezhnev and Prime Minister Nikolai Tikhonov announced their intention to proceed with a synthetic fuels program at the Twenty-sixth Party Congress in February 1981, utilizing

Kansk-Achinsk lignites for conversion to liquid fuel. Both electricity from the mine sites and liquids are planned for mid-1980s production.[38]

Soviet interest in this area spans a wide range of alternative and renewable technologies: gas hydrates in the permafrost zones of the Arctic, especially offshore; nuclear-fusion power by means of the tokamak reactor for toroidal containment; solar cells (including very small-scale 3-5 MW solar towers under construction in the Crimea and construction of a much larger 5,000 MW solar-power facility also in the Crimea); tidal, wind, and geothermal power (including studies of 1000 MW geothermal power stations); magnetohydrodynamic (MHD) technology, for the conversion of heat into electricity by way of turbine generators; and energy from biofuels, particularly the formation of methane.[39] Although not classified as alternative energy sources, peat, firewood, and hydroelectricity contribute between 5 and 6 percent of the Soviet primary energy mix.

Geothermal energy and synfuels could make a small contribution by 1990 if sufficient money is allocated. The volcanic Kamchatka Peninsula, southern Siberia, the North Caucasus, and Georgia in Transcaucasia appear to hold sufficient promise for small-scale applications (on the order of 200 MW power stations rather than 1,000 MW as suggested in Soviet studies). Such applications include electricity generation, space heating, greenhouse, and balneological (mineral spas) use.[40]

A major synfuels effort is probably beyond domestic Soviet capabilities. West Germany has shown interest in assisting Soviet coal-liquids and coal-gas development; agreement is all but certain for the delivery of advanced coal-processing facilities to be used in the Kansk-Achinsk basin.[41] With German assistance, a small synfuels industry could begin turning out liquid fuels as early as the mid-1980s.

A. Sheindlin, chairman of the Coordinating Council on Synthetic Fuel, has pushed for the expenditure of 30 billion rubles (about $41 billion) over the next ten years for a wide-scale effort producing 100 million tons (2 mmbdoe) of coal liquids.[42] It is doubtful that his proposal will be accepted or that a Soviet synfuels industry could produce 100 million tons of coal liquids per year the early 1990s. The costs of conventional-fuels extraction, processing, and distribution (including construction) probably will be favored over synthetic alternatives.

Current Soviet programs include catalytic hydrogenation, high-speed pyrolysis, and direct burning of shale for generation of electricity. More than eighty shale deposits totaling 190 billion tons of estimated proven reserves have been identified on Soviet territory.[43] Soviet efforts in shale conversions can be expected to continue, but it remains unclear whether coal-liquids manufacture will receive more attention than shale programs.

Problems in Energy Consumption

At the June 1980 CMEA meeting and again at the Twenty-sixth Party Congress in February 1981, the USSR pledged to increase its energy deliveries to Eastern Europe by 20 percent during the Eleventh Five Year Plan. Of the scheduled increase, 16.5 percent was to be oil and gas exports; the remaining 3.5 percent was planned as electricity shipments.[44]

It now appears likely that the 1985 commitments cannot be kept. Moscow has cut oil exports to Eastern Europe, with the exception of Poland, by 10 percent. If this holds to 1985, Eastern Europe will receive 1.44 mmbd (72 million tons) instead of the planned 1.6 mmbd (80 million tons). The planned natural-gas substitution for oil in the USSR and additional mid-decade hard-currency gas exports to Western Europe will prevent much of an increase in gas exports to Eastern Europe. Delays in coal production and nuclear-electricity generation may force the Soviets to reconsider fuel switching (out of oil) and, while 1985 electricity exports to CMEA-Europe could be met, 1990 targets probably will fall short. The planned 20 percent growth in energy exports to 1985 could very well be cut by half or more.

Conservation now figures prominently in all bloc plans. "Stricter consumption norms" in the USSR will be "reinforced by a system of heavy surcharges in the event of over-consumption and of substantial bonuses if greater economies are achieved than had been projected." The new norms are intended for industry, residential, and power sources.[45] Yet it is easier to set administrative norms than to enforce them. According to Leslie Dienes, such norms "are set entirely by trial and error" through bureaucratic bargaining. Residential units already pay "a far higher unit rate than industrial and commercial consumers," so it is unlikely that the stricter norms will achieve much. The lack of meters in household units will make regulation still more difficult.[46]

Industry is largely responsible for the difficulties the Soviet bloc has encountered in reducing energy demand. Over three-fifths of Soviet consumption and one-half of East European consumption goes toward industrial development.[47] The focus on output cannot be more than marginally altered by introduction of stricter consumption norms in a system that stresses plan fulfillment and extensive growth. Energy-efficiency improvements, especially in Eastern Europe, will be expensive and will include greater movement from solid to liquid fuels, which may not be available on world markets at affordable prices.

Expansion of cogeneration and district heating has slowed considerably in CMEA owing to excessive reliance on solid-fuels supply, which is becoming scarcer. Until nuclear-power plants are built to cogenerate heat and power and district heating, continued growth from this source cannot be assumed. In this regard, it will take at least a decade for significant inroads to be made in Eastern Europe and longer in the Soviet Union.[48]

Dienes argues that the "substitution of hydrocarbons for solid fuels has basically come to an end" and that "given the very slow retirement rate characteristic of the Soviet capital stock and the rapidly worsening accessibility of natural resources which demands rising energy input, further technical advances to improve energy efficiency will be slower than in the past."[49] Both trends imply a worsening of the energy-GNP ratio and a decline in the efficient utilization of energy resources, for increased hard-coal and lignite conversions to electricity (planned for throughout CMEA but especially in the USSR, Poland, and the GDR) will require greater fuels input per end-use energy and industrial output. Conservation in the USSR is hampered by the small amounts of fuel currently allocated to the household-municipal and private-transportation sectors, about one-fifth or less of aggregate energy consumption.[50] Any savings here would register insignificant national gains and may contribute to greater social discontent.

In Eastern Europe, the structural rigidities caused by continued reliance on extensive use of subbituminous coal (mostly lignite) will hamper industrial modernization plans. Plans to increase domestic coal utilization may grant the bloc greater autonomy but will also "require huge capital investments in machinery and transportation facilities, impede efforts to make production processes more energy efficient, and intensify already high levels of air and water pollution."[51]

Therefore, conservation and/or fuel switching where feasible in Eastern Europe and the Soviet Union will not alter the growing gap between supply of primary and secondary energy commodities and attendant demand. Lacking sufficient indigenous energy resources and subject to ever-mounting debt, Eastern Europe will have limited ability to enter world markets and purchase OPEC-priced oil. Examples of individual bloc-country problems presented next illustrate the high degree of dependence the Warsaw Pact allies exhibit toward the USSR for their energy needs.

Hungary and Czechoslovakia embarked on a joint project with Yugoslavia in the 1970s to construct the Adria crude-oil pipeline, planned to import 5 million tons (100,000 b/d) annually of OPEC crude. The pipeline was completed in 1979, but oil has yet to be imported through the pipeline. The second oil shock set off by the revolution in Iran sent oil prices to record levels. Additional OPEC oil became unaffordable at post-1979 prices.

The non-Soviet bloc partners together imported about 20 percent of their crude from OPEC at the close of the 1970s, a percentage that will probably decline. Eastern Europe's share of manufactured products imported by OPEC, always small, will continue to shrink.[52] While Rumania alone maintains a sizable crude import trade with OPEC for its petrochemical industry and refined-product export trade, Rumania's projected multibillion-dollar trade deficits with OPEC may force it to scale back its trade and domestic economic commitments.

Thirty percent of the GDR's export earnings must be used for payment of the oil-import bill; the country's debt-service ratio (the ratio of interest and debt repayment to hard-currency earnings) exceeds 40 percent. With declining levels of resource imports from the Soviet Union across the board, particularly oil, the GDR will have difficulty in coming up with enough foreign exchange to buy energy and commodity resources for hard currency. The East German industrial base, now aging and inefficient, is relied upon by other CMEA allies for higher-caliber goods.[53]

Czechoslovakia currently is experiencing delays in its nuclear-power program. Brown-coal production fell again in 1981, with a concomitant decline in steel output. Plans for growth in national income to 1985 have been cut from the original 14 to 16 percent increase to 10 to 14 percent. As prices for Soviet crude have increased, deliveries have been reduced, necessitating a 12 to 13 percent cutback in oil products delivered to industrial and residential consumers. There are also some reports that Soviet natural-gas exports of 8.4 bcm may be partially curtailed in the near future,[54] but it is more likely that Czechoslovakia's role as a transit route for the Soviet export pipeline to Western Europe will enable Prague to increase Soviet gas imports. Hard-currency constraints force Czech planners to allocate money for current consumption rather than energy-efficiency improvements, a choice that in turn impedes progress in making Czech goods competitive in Western markets.

Postwar Rumania traditionally has combined a relatively independent foreign policy in a tightly controlled political and economic setting. The outer parameters of Rumanian foreign-policy experimentation may now have been reached, with the long-term decline in Rumanian oil production limiting President Nicolae Ceausescu's options. Coal production fell short of planned targets as well, and Rumania's hard-currency debt now stands at about $10 billion and could reach $16 billion by the end of 1982 if hard-currency borrowing is not stopped (hinted at by Ceausescu in June 1981).[55] Borrowing from the West has been used largely to finance OPEC crude-oil imports, which are then refined into petroleum products for export to Western Europe. Western lenders are now alarmed at the prospect of another debt crisis in Eastern Europe and have indicated that future large-scale, long-term loans to Rumania are in serious doubt. Most-favored-nation status and membership in the International Monetary Fund somewhat mitigate Rumania's problems, but CMEA difficulties and commitments could nullify these effects. The Soviets, for example, seem to regard Rumania as capable of fending for itself. Rumania has been refused additional oil exports from the Soviet Union despite an offer to pay world prices rather than transferable rubles for the crude.[56]

Both Bulgaria and Hungary have been forced to scale back domestic spending. Despite the sheltered nature of the Bulgarian economy, the bulk of Bulgaria's oil consumption comes from Soviet imports, the long-term future of which remain uncertain. Conservation and efficiency improvements, as in other bloc countries, will be relied upon to make up any shortfall, and as in other bloc countries, official pronouncements about raising productivity and lowering the energy-GNP elasticity will prove extremely difficult to implement. Bulgaria is the most oil-intensive CMEA economy next to the USSR and will face large refinery reinvestment costs with a change in Sofia's energy strategy.[57]

Hungary embarked on its New Economic Mechanism (NEM) in 1968, attempting to decentralize economic decision making, rationalize prices based more on inputs and demand, and open up the economy to foreign trade and investment through the introduction of an improved exchange-rate system. The opening to the West and the economic liberalization placed Hungary in a tight squeeze, for the recession in the OECD nations and the two oil shocks of the 1970s resulted in a worsening of Hungary's terms of trade and an escalation of its hard-currency debt (the debt-service ratio is now placed at over 40 percent) with the industrialized West. Should the oil exports promised to Hungary by the USSR in the current five-year period remain at the low 1980 level, Hungary's growth rate would fall below 1 percent, an unacceptably low level of economic growth compared to the much-better rates of the 1970s.[58]

The rise of the Solidarity movement in Poland, beginning in August 1980, coincided with a worsening economic situation, which forced the government of Edward Gierek to raise food prices. Detractors of the movement pointed to the breakdown in socialist labor discipline as evidenced by falling coal and industrial production throughout 1981. Coal output dropped 16 percent, while hard-currency coal exports were cut in half from 1980 levels.

Hard-currency debt continued to climb toward the $30 billion mark when the military crackdown of December 13, 1981, placed future Western loans and credits in jeopardy. Poland was spared the reduction in Soviet oil deliveries visited upon the other bloc countries but faces such massive industrial, efficiency, and debt problems that above-quota shipments may be necessary. It is far from certain that the Jaruzelski regime will be able to raise productivity, as its leadership claims. Protracted strife probably will be the price paid for failure to accommodate church and Solidarity demands and reforms. The drain on an already-strained Soviet economy and the economically adverse ripple effects now being witnessed in the other CMEA states could prove too damaging for a sustained Soviet bloc effort, especially should the West clamp down on further extension of loans.

How long can Moscow continue to supply a grossly inefficient Polish economy, which could require, according to I.D. Kozlov of the Soviet Union, 1.4 mmbd (70 million tons) and 40 bcm per year (the amount initially envisaged for supply to Western Europe via the Siberian export line) of natural gas by 2000?[59] By then, Polish imports of Soviet oil at that magnitude would comprise well over one-tenth of Soviet oil production, an inordinately large share, which would leave little for remaining bloc consumption and nothing for hard-currency export. In this regard, the lack of exploratory activity off Vietnam and the projected rise of Cuban oil demand (to 280,000 b/d, 14 million tons, or more by 1985) will force non-European CMEA needs to be met increasingly by Soviet supply on soft terms. Today communist Indochina (Vietnam, Laos, and Kampuchea) imports 80 percent of its oil from the USSR at $5 to $7 per barrel.[60] These terms will surely be reassessed as Moscow's oil supply tightens.

Looking across fuel types, then, and at individual bloc countries' consumption patterns, one can establish the close link between the extensive-growth model exemplified by the Soviet and East European systems and the rate of energy growth in the determination of national income. The high energy-GNP correlation, the lack of interfuel flexibility (particularly in Eastern Europe), and the dim prospects for lasting structural conservation and demand restraint undoubtedly will result in very low or negative economic-growth rates in the 1980s.

These links help clarify the importance attached to intra-CMEA fuels trade by the smaller bloc countries. Ironically, the priority accorded long-term agricultural and industrial modernization and diversification in order to enhance economic efficiency—one method of reducing the dependence on external energy sources—will increase demand for hydrocarbon inputs.[61] The lower-than-world prices charged in most CMEA trade transactions, especially for oil, do not encourage conservation of resources or efficiency of operation. The failure of the CMEA pricing mechanism to factor in higher Soviet fuels recovery or transportation costs poses a dilemma similar to that experienced in the United States under its price-control regime: the true economic cost of oil utilization is not reflected through price, resulting in misallocation and waste.[62]

Wholesale price increases in raw materials for industrial processes or final-product increases in the urban consumer sector will not achieve that which a comprehensive planning and price revision might. There are far too many rigidities in the Soviet economy, which will undermine changes short of significant reform. In the words of a Soviet state energy inspector, "The root of the evil lies in the fact that enterprises are allocated resources according to their needs rather than according to norms of consumption per unit of output."[63] Increasing the cost of energy inputs in the Soviet construction industry, in other words, will not by itself alter that industry's 30 percent higher energy consumption per unit of output compared with the U.S. construction industry.[64] The same could be said of steel, metallurgy, and most other heavy industries as well.[65]

Soviet subsidies to Eastern Europe will place a further strain on the Soviet economy, which in turn will direct rubles away from costly investments in energy efficiency and conservation. The upward trend (from an average of $6 billion per year in the mid-to-late 1970s to at least $21 billion in 1980) in direct and indirect subsidies to Eastern Europe constitutes an important element in Soviet security policy but will adversely affect bloc willingness to attempt to restructure their economies away from the Soviet model.[66]

The 1980s, therefore, will severely challenge and strain the Soviet bloc. The future availability of oil on soft terms is in serious doubt, and delays or shortfalls in remaining Soviet hydrocarbon exports and CMEA conservation and substitution programs probably will result in intrabloc competition for scarce resources. The potential for political conflict and heightened tension will grow as individual leadership elites and their populations try to cope with stagnating economies made worse by energy crises. The impetus to look abroad in search of alternative solutions to worsening bloc-wide problems may become irresistible as the Soviet determination to proceed with the natural-gas pipeline to Western Europe indicates. Whether the USSR looks south toward the Persian Gulf or remains fixed on rapprochement with the West will be determined in large part by the CMEA's energy future.

Notes

1. Jonathan P. Stern, "Western Forecasts of Soviet and East European Energy over the Next Two Decades (1980-2000)," in U.S. Congress, Joint Economic Committee, *Energy in Soviet Policy*, p. 32 (hereafter referred to as JEC(1)).

2. John Hannigan and Carl McMillan, "Joint Investment in Resource Development: Sectoral Approaches to Socialist Integration," U.S. Congress, Joint Economic Committee, *East European Economic Assessment: Part 2-Regional Assessments*, July 10, 1981 (hereaffter referred to as JEC(2)).

3. "Soviet Gas Goals Called Unattainable," *Oil and Gas Journal*, January 25, 1981, p. 360. B. Trofimov of the Tyumen provincial party committee recently complained of persistent infrastructural problems, noting that the Ministry of Transport Construction's failure to build a road will keep transportation from the gasfields at 20 percent below capacity. "Shortcomings in West Siberia," *Petroleum Economist*, November 1982, p. 466.

4. Stern, "Western Forecasts," p. 30.

5. Ibid., pp. 34-35.

6. James Ellis, "Warsaw Pact Energy Prospects: Implications for the West," *NATO Review* (April 1981):30. Ellis sees consumption "growing at about the same rate as production," which is given as 7 percent.

7. J.B. Hannigan and C.H. McMillan, *The Energy Factor in Soviet-East European Relations* (Ottawa: Institute of Soviet and East European Studies, Carleton University, September 1981), pp. 39-41.

8. Ibid., p. 1.

9. Tony Scanlan, "Outlook for Soviet Oil" (paper presented at Conference on Oil and Money in the Eighties, London, September 1981), p. 17; Hannigan and McMillan, *Energy Factor*, p. 43.

10. Ibid., p. 8.

11. Friedmann Muller, "The Energy Sector Status of the Soviet Union with an Eye to the 1980s," *Soviet and Eastern European Foreign Trade* (Spring 1980):13.

12. Hannigan and McMillan, *Energy Factor*, p. 30.

13. Stern, "Western Forecasts," p. 35. *Business Week* has placed Soviet coal reserves at 89 billion metric tons: 80 billion hard coal and 9 billion lignite. "German Technology Teams up with Soviet Coal," *Business Week*, November 30, 1981, p. 79.

14. "World Status: Coal Trade," *Energy Economist* (February 1982):11.

15. The GDR used lignite for 60 percent of basic energy requirements in 1980. The current Five Year Plan calls for a further increase in this percentage, to be used "increasingly to replace mineral oils as feedstocks in the expanding chemical industry." However, investment costs per ton of production will double. "News in Brief," *Petroleum Economist* (June 1981):270.

16. Thane Gustafson, "Energy and the Soviet Bloc," *International Security* (Winter 1981-1982):70-71.

17. John M. Kramer, "The Policy Dilemmas of East Europe's Energy Gap," in JEC(2), p. 472.

18. Gustafson, "Energy," pp. 71-72.

19. Kevin Klose, "Discontent Seething in Soviet Mines," *Washington Post*, January 30, 1981, pp. A1, A18. Soviet nonfuel mineral development suffers from similar problems: "declining ore grades in existing mines, obsolete technology, insufficient investment in new facilities and the inability to raise mineral production with increased labor." "Soviet Mine Woes Cited," *New York Times*, December 7, 1981, p. D9.

20. Theodore Shabad, "News Notes," *Soviet Geography* (April 1982): 288.

21. U.S. Congress, Office of Technology Assessment (OTA), *Technology and Soviet Energy Availability* (November 1981), p. 151; Stern, "Western Forecasts," p. 36.

22. Theodore Shabad, "Strip-Mine Development in Eastern Regions Pressed," *Soviet Geography* (December 1981):688. The Communist Party

Central Committee and the USSR Council of Ministers recently adopted a resolution on open-cut (strip-mine) coal mining in which nearly every ministry involved with coal production, construction of facilities, and coal-electricity generation was accused of "lagging." For example, "The U.S.S.R. Ministry of the Coal Industry and the U.S.S.R. Ministry of Power and Electrification are behind schedule in commissioning production capacities at opencut coal mines and the thermal power stations that are being built to burn coal from those mines; they have not provided for the priority creation of enterprises and facilities of the construction-industry base; and they have not fulfilled assignments for constructing residential buildings and municipal-service, cultural and consumer-service facilities and opening them, for occupancy and operation." "Steps Planned to Boost Coal Production," *Current Digest of the Soviet Press*, November 4, 1981, p. 13, citing "In Opencut Mines," *Pravda*, October 4, 1981, p. 1, and "In the CPSU Central Committee and the U.S.S.R. Council of Ministers," *Izvestia*, October 4, 1981, pp. 1-2.

23. Hannigan and McMillan, *Energy Factor*, p. 29; "Soviet Nuclear Energy: How Soon Will They Meet Their Goals?" *Business and Trade*, September 7, 1981, p. 7; Jim Harding, "Soviet Nuclear Setbacks," *Social Science and Modern Society* (July-August 1981):73.

24. Hannigan and McMillan, *Energy Factor*, p. 42.

25. Gustafson, "Energy," p. 74; Hannigan and McMillan, *Energy Factor*, pp. 28-29.

26. Gustafson, "Energy," p. 75.

27. "Incredible Entanglements Impede Czech Projects," *Energy Economist* (February 1982):8; Gustafson, "Energy," p. 77, lists the planned cutback as 7,280 MW.

28. "Incredible Entanglements," p. 8.

29. Gustafson, "Energy," pp. 77-78.

30. Theodore Shabad, "High-Level Conference Highlights Soviet Nuclear Power Program," *Soviet Geography* (September 1981):446.

31. J.F. Pilat, "Communist Nuclear Practice," *Social Science and Modern Society* (July-August 1981):12. Pilat, quoting Frank Barnaby of the Stockholm International Peace Research Institute, claims that only 5,000 MW are scheduled each year by the end of the 1980s and 10,000 MW each year by the end of the 1990s. Current plans, however, call for an increase in new capacity of 10 million kilowatts per year (10,000 MW) by the end of the 1980s. P. Neporozhny, USSR Minister of Power and Electrification, "Power Engineering in the Forefront: The Five Year Plan's Peaceful Atom," *Pravda*, June 4, 1981, p. 2, cited by "Soviet Nuclear Power Plans Outlined," *Current Digest of the Soviet Press*, July 1, 1981, p. 6.

32. "Soviet Nuclear Energy," p. 7; Kevin Klose, "Reactor Complex in Cossack Country Girds to Power Soviet Future," *Washington Post*, October

17, 1980, p. A23. John Hardt similarly suggests there may be "serious difficulties . . . encountered" in the Soviet nuclear-power program. John P. Hardt, "Soviet and East European Energy Policy: Security Implications" (paper presented at Conference on the Future of Nuclear Power, Federal Republic of Germany, December 1981).

33. Zhores Medvedev, *Nuclear Disaster in the Urals*, trans. George Saunders (New York: W.W. Norton, 1979), and "Soviet Nuclear Energy," p. 7. The recent interest in environmental protection was highlighted at the mid-1981 Conference on the Eleventh Five Year Plan (see notes 30 and 31). The relative safety advantages of nuclear plants compared with fossil-fuel plants were also stressed: "Atomic power stations do not pollute the water or the air. . . . Special studies have shown that environmental pollution by harmful emissions (including radioactive emissions) is many times greater from thermal power stations than it is from atomic power stations." "Soviet Nuclear Power Plans Outlined," p. 6.

34. Gustafson, "Energy," p. 77.

35. Neporozhny, "Power Engineering," p. 6. A. Aleksandrov, president of the Soviet Academy of Sciences, "stressed the need for improvements in the automation of power station equipment, and the need to ensure the uninterrupted operation of nuclear stations, implying that there had been several shut-downs." "Russia's Nuclear Power Trouble," *Economist Foreign Report*, August 13, 1981, p. 6.

36. OTA, *Technology*, pp. 156-158.

37. Ibid., p. 9.

38. Theodore Shabad, "Soviet Announces a Synthetic Fuels Program," *Soviet Geography* (May 1981):341.

39. B.A. Rahmer, "Russia Looks for Alternatives," *Petroleum Economist* (November 1981):467-468; Theodore Shabad, "Construction of Solar Power Station Starts," *Soviet Geography* (November 1981):615; I. Berezin and Ye. Pantskhava, "Prospects for Biotechnology," *Ekonomicheskaya gazeta* (July 1981), translated in "Rosy Future for Biofuel Industry Seen," *Current Digest of the Soviet Press*, October 21, 1981, pp. 12, 14.

40. Theodore Shabad, "Geothermal Station in Kamchatka Expanded," *Soviet Geography* (May 1981):342; Philip R. Pryde, "Geothermal Energy Development in the Soviet Union," *Soviet Geography* (February 1979):69-81.

41. John Tagliaube, "German Coal Plant Deal Expected with Soviet," *New York Times*, September 19, 1981, p. 29.

42. Rahmer, "Russia Looks for Alternatives," p. 468.

43. U.S. Department of Defense, *United States versus Soviet Synthetic Fuels Technology Assessment*, Report of an Ad Hoc Task Force under the sponsorship of the Office of the Under Secretary of Defense for Research and Engineering (1981).

44. Hannigan and McMillan, *Energy Factor*, p. 33.

45. "News in Brief: U.S.S.R.," *Petroleum Economist* (August 1981): 359.

46. Leslie Dienes, "Energy Conservation in the U.S.S.R.," in JEC(1), pp. 116-117.

47. Leslie Dienes and Nikos Economou, "Comecon Energy Demand in the 1980s: A Sectoral Analysis," in *CMEA: Energy 1980-1990* (Brussels: NATO Economics Directorate, April 8-10, 1981), p. 40.

48. Ibid., p. 43.

49. Dienes, "Energy Conservation," p. 104.

50. Ibid., p. 108. About two-thirds of Soviet oil and gas consumption was used in power plants. Coal and gas together "cannot be expected to cover all boiler requirements before the end of the 1980s. Except for coke, furnaces will continue to depend on hydrocarbons to an overwhelming extent, with return to solid fuels infeasible . . . the role of nuclear power . . . in saving oil and gas in this century will be small" (pp. 106-107).

51. Kramer, "Policy Dilemmas," p. 474.

52. Ronald G. Oechsler and John A. Martens, "East European Trade with OPEC: A Solution to Emerging Energy Problems?" in JEC(2).

53. *East European Statistical Service*, 24 (July-August 1981), p. 4; "Trade between the GDR and the USSR in the Light of Reduced Growth," *Soviet and Eastern European Foreign Trade* (Spring 1981):21-41; John M. Geddes, "East Germany: Hard Times Ahead," *Wall Street Journal*, February 24, 1982, p. 35.

54. B.A. Rahmer, "Czechoslovakia: 'Unparalleled' Economic Problems," *Petroleum Economist* (February 1982):53-54. Czechoslovakia feels particularly squeezed by the Polish crisis and will not be able to spend hard currency buying the 2 million tons (40,000 b/d) of oil curtailed by the USSR. See Michael Dobbs, "Burdened Soviets Plan to Cut Back Energy Sales to Eastern Bloc by 10%," *Washington Post*, December 11, 1981, pp. 1, 34, and Henry Kamm, "Czech Leaders Are Nervous about the Crisis in Poland," *New York Times*, January 8, 1982, p. A8.

55. F. Stephen Larrabee, "Instability and Change in Eastern Europe," *International Security* (Winter 1981-1982):42.

56. "Oil Country Hot Line: Soviets Say No to Rumania," *World Oil* (September 1981):9.

57. "Eastern Europe: Dwindling Supplies," *Petroleum Economist* (January 1982):28; Dienes and Economou, "Comecon Energy Demand," p. 19.

58. John M. Starrels, "The Prospect of Less Soviet Oil for Eastern Europe," *Wall Street Journal*, February 11, 1982, p. 28. Growth in Hungarian net material product averaged over 6 percent in the early 1970s and over 3 percent in the late 1970s.

59. Gustafson, "Energy," p. 73.

60. Jeffrey Segal, "Indochina: Energy Dependence on USSR," *Petroleum Economist* (September 1981):377-379.

61. R.T. Maddock, "Oil and Economic Growth in the Soviet Union," *Three Banks Review* (March 1980):31.

62. Hannigan and McMillan, *Energy Factor*, pp. 18-19.

63. S. Moiseyenko, "Permit Me to Punish You," *Pravda*, December 15, 1980, p. 3, in *Current Digest of the Soviet Press*, January 14, 1981, p. 20.

64. Maddock, "Oil and Economic Growth," p. 32.

65. A. Lalayants, Gosplan vice-chairman, admitted in regard to conservation: "It must be said frankly that the structure of the production of pig iron, steel and rolled metal is still far from the optimal level that it can and must reach." A. Lalayants, "Urgent Questions of Fuel Conservation," *Izvestia*, November 15, 1981, p. 2, in "Planner Lists Ways of Conserving Energy," *Current Digest of the Soviet Press*, December 16, 1981, p. 16.

66. Jan Vanous and Michael Marrese, "Soviet Subsidies to Eastern Economies," *Wall Street Journal*, January 15, 1982, p. 24. The DIA cites a 1980 subsidy level of $24 billion (see chapter one).

4 The Siberian Gas Pipeline: Implications for the West

During the Tenth Five Year Plan (1976-1980), 30,000 kilometers of natural-gas pipelines were laid down in the Soviet Union. The Eleventh Five Year Plan (1981-1985) calls for 48,000 kilometers of trunk gas lines to be built, including six major lines from West Siberia to the European USSR. One of these six lines will connect Urengoi in northwestern Siberia with Uzhgorod on the Soviet-Czech border, and from there will link up with Czech and existing West European gas networks.

The proposed Siberian export line to West Europe has created transatlantic discord and controversy. The merits of the gas-for-pipe deal were hotly debated in 1981 and 1982 and inevitably became enmeshed in the NATO deliberations concerning the response to Poland's martial-law decision of December 13, 1981.

The Siberian Gas-Export Line

The project as initially envisaged in 1978 called for completion on Soviet territory of a natural-gas pipeline to run from Yamburg north of the Arctic Circle, south through Urengoi, and then across thousands of miles of land to Uzhgorod. Transfer stations at the West German-Czech border and at the Austrian-Czech border would then pump the gas to West Germany, Austria, France, Italy, the Netherlands, Belgium, Switzerland, and possibly Spain. Throughput capacity was placed at 40 billion cubic meters (bcm) per year, which would have raised West European reliance on Soviet natural-gas imports from approximately 25 bcm in 1981 to about 65 bcm by the late 1980s. Eastern Europe was originally scheduled to receive an additional 10 bcm per year, raising its level to over 40 bcm of annual Soviet gas imports. An amortization period of between eight and ten years at an interest rate of 7.8 to 8.5 percent following completion of the pipeline was requested by Soyuzgasexport, the Soviet gas-trading firm. Initial exports of natural gas were projected to net $8 billion to $10 billion per year in hard currencies.

Since the initial series of negotiations, undertaken separately with each state's utility consortium, the project has been scaled back. The natural-gas deposit at Yamburg on the Taz Peninsula holds a reserve base sufficient to supply Western Europe's contracted needs for many years, but inadequate infrastructural development caused the Soviet Gas Ministry and Gosplan to shift their focus south to Urgengoi in mid-1981. The Yamburg development has now been put off until later in the 1980s.

Urengoi is the world's largest single gas complex in operation today, containing between 6 trillion and 7 tcm of reserves, accounting for roughly 20 percent of Soviet gas reserves and about 7 percent of world proved reserves. The five largest gas fields in northern Tyumen Oblast (including Urengoi) have reserves of close to 20 tcm, about two-thirds of total Soviet gas reserves.

The increment to planned natural-gas production—195 bcm (435 bcm produced in 1980 subtracted from 630 bcm projected for 1985)—is expected to come entirely from Urengoi, scheduled to grow from an annual production of 50 bcm in 1980 to 250 bcm in 1985. But many Western energy analysts believe that this projection was too great even for the successful Soviet natural-gas industry. Should Urengoi production come close to meeting the planned targets, bottlenecks in transporting the gas from West Siberia to the European USSR will prevent full utilization of Urengoi's capacity, especially for growing domestic use and oil-substitution programs. Diversion of resources toward the West European-bound export line undoubtedly will result in still-greater delays in domestic gas-consumption plans.

For example, the installation of compressor stations typically lags far behind pipe laying.[1] The technical capacity to mass produce reliable 16 MW and 25 MW gas turbines domestically is currently lacking, despite vocal Soviet pronouncements to the contrary. During most of 1982, it was thought that the timely importation of the turbines and component parts may be indefinitely delayed because of the Reagan administration's decision to forbid the sale (and the use of previously delivered sales) of General Electric rotors, nozzles, and stator blades to that firm's European manufacturing associates. Although this is no longer a problem, the construction of 3,400 miles of the natural-gas export pipeline, traversing permafrost, mountains, bogs, swamps, and over 700 rivers and streams, and the rapid fulfillment of the Urengoi plan (which is the primary gas-expansion program through 1985) still hold the key to the success or failure of the Soviet Eleventh Five Year Energy Plan.

Thus far, only four governments have ratified their participation. The Italian gas distributor SNAM has negotiated the details, but the government announced a "pause for reflection" following the Polish martial-law decision.

Table 4-1 shows the states slated to receive additional Soviet gas shipments for twenty to twenty-five years beginning in 1984 via the Siberian export line. A range of 38.5 to 40.5 bcm of gas exports was thus projected, plus annual delivery of 700 million cubic meters to West Berlin. By the spring of 1982, however, the Netherlands' Gasunie (the Dutch gas distributor)

Table 4-1
Planned Soviet Pipeline Exports to End of 1981
(bcm/year)

West Germany	10.5
France	8
Italy	8
Belgium	5
Netherlands	3-4
Austria	3-5
Switzerland	1

announced it would cut its share to 2 bcm and possibly eliminate participation altogether. Belgium's Distrigaz said it would probably take only 2 to 3 bcm and might buy even less because of the Soviet refusal to offer Belgian companies any equipment contracts. Austria announced in February 1982 that it may halve the initial import level because of price increases, recession, and a 5 to 6 percent decline in natural-gas consumption in 1981. If Italy dropped out, it was then thought that the reduced import levels from the Siberian project would total only 25 to 27.5 bcm (see table 4-2).

Belgium and the Netherlands subsequently decided not to participate, further reducing the total to 21 to 22.5 bcm and thereby cutting Soviet hard-currency earnings nearly in half. Spain's participation could total 2 bcm per year, but its involvement is too uncertain to include in the revised estimates. Offtake valves reportedly are planned for installation along the Czech transit route in order to provide an undisclosed amount of additional gas to Eastern Europe. As of August 1982, only four of the original governments had ratified yearly gas-supply agreements: West Germany at 10.5 bcm, France at 6.4 to 8 bcm; Austria at 1.5 bcm with an option to purchase an additional 1 bcm, and Switzerland at 0.36 bcm.

The construction arrangement is a compensation package originally projected to cost $10 billion to $15 billion. The cost escalation associated with unforeseen problems and delays pushes some final cost estimates to between $20 billion and $30 billion, with certain estimates (such as Senator Jake Garn's of Utah) ranging as high as $45 billion. Critics argue that when the trans-Alaskan crude-oil pipeline was built in the mid-1970s, the cost of each one-hundred miles of construction averaged about $1 billion. With relative efficiencies of construction and organization taken into account, opponents assert, a total figure of $45 billion for the Soviet pipeline is not unduly high. It is, however, difficult to see how the total foreign-currency costs for the entire gas-distribution system (all six pipelines) could exceed $25 billion, including Soviet labor costs and imports of steel pipe and compressor stations.

Table 4-2
Revised Soviet Pipeline Exports, Spring 1982
(bcm/year)

West Germany	10.5
France	8
Belgium	2-3
Netherlands	2
Austria	1.5-3
Switzerland	1

Ruhrgas-AG of the Federal Republic of Germany (FRG), the principal German gas utility and distributor, led a German-buying consortium, including Thyssengas, Gelsenberg (BP), Salzgitter Ferngas, and Gewerkschaft Brigitta-Elwerath, in negotiating the delivered-price formula for the new Soviet gas. The French and Italian gas consortia followed suit after Ruhrgas achieved a price of $4.75 per million British thermal units (Btu), about the heat-generation equivalent of 1,000 cubic feet of natural gas. The French achieved a delivered-price schedule of $4.52 to $4.62 per million Btu. Both the French and German payments are to be made in their own currencies (centimes per kWh and pfennigs per kWh, respectively), with the contracts to run for twenty to twenty-five years.

The new contracts thus shield the French and Germans from a fluctuating dollar. There is, however, a price escalator, a formula linked to price increases in each market in light fuel (heating) oil (40 percent), heavy fuel oil (40 percent), and a basket of crude oils (20 percent).[2] The 1984 floor price is estimated to be $5.50 per million Btu.

A consortium of West German banks is financing the Soviet purchase of the compressor stations, fifty-six-inch large-diameter pipe, pipe-laying equipment, and related materials and services. The German consortium extended an initial credit of $2 billion for the Soviet foreign-trade enterprises to purchase pipeline-related equipment. The pipe orders are to be purchased separately on a yearly basis.

Germany's Mannesmann Anlagenbau, a plant-construction subsidiary of the giant Mannesmann steel concern, and Creusot-Loire of France, a major French steel company, have formed a joint venture in the building and installation of twenty-two gas-compressor stations valued at close to $1 billion (in 1981 dollars). Mannesmann will also deliver related compressor equipment (piping systems, skids, pumps) worth $60 million and over $2 billion of steel pipe. Eventually a total of forty-one compressor stations will be operating along the length of the pipeline, the remaining nineteen stations to be supplied by Nuovo Pignone, an Italian government holding company that is part of ENI, the Italian national energy firm.

AEG-Kanis, a subsidiary of the West German electrical firm AEG-Telefunken, is scheduled to deliver forty-seven compressor turbines, another twenty-one gas turbines will be supplied by John Brown & Company of Scotland, and fifty-seven turbines are to be supplied by Nuovo Pignone. AEG-Kanis probably will win contracts for electrical control components, communications, and remote-control systems.

French, Dutch, and Belgian banks also extended lines of credit to the USSR for purchase of French, Dutch, and Belgian equipment, but no Belgian or Dutch companies were given any pipeline-related business, which explains Belgian and Dutch reticence in importing Soviet gas. In addition to Creusot-Loire, a major French computer firm (Thomson-CSF) will supply at least $300 million worth of advanced computer-monitoring equipment.

In sum, the construction of a 3,400-mile natural-gas pipeline from northwest Siberia through Czechoslovakia to Western Europe, carrying a projected supply of some 20 to 30 bcm per year of natural gas beginning in the later 1980s (the 1984 gas deliveries are scheduled to build slowly toward capacity after several years or more), is all but assured. The Soviets have begun preliminary construction along the proposed route, and the Europeans remain committed to the project's completion. Could the sanctions imposed by the United States have frustrated or delayed the Siberian pipeline?

American Sanctions, Round One

The U.S. sanctions imposed by President Ronald Reagan after martial law was declared in Poland fell under the heading of foreign-policy controls, a form of export controls separate from national security controls. Both foreign-policy and national-security controls previously applied to U.S. oil and gas equipment sales to the USSR in the refining, distribution, drilling, and exploration sectors. Technology transfers of proprietary know-how in these sectors and the processing sector as well are disallowed under preexisting national-security controls.[3] U.S. energy-technology trade with the Soviet Union has never been very great, and while the "U.S. is the sole or preferred supplier in a number of areas, including integrated computer systems and software, submersible pumps, blow-out preventers and tertiary recovery techniques," Moscow has decided to buy elsewhere when feasible because of the American penchant to politicize trade with the Soviet bloc.[4]

AEG-Kanis, along with John Brown & Company and Nuovo Pignone, are to supply 125 turbines for the forty-one compressor stations along the Siberian export line. The head station contains five Frame-3 10 MW turbines, and the remaining forty stations will house three 25 MW turbines: one for daily operations, one for reserve, and one for maintenance purposes. As manufacturing associates of General Electric (the U.S. firm denied Commerce Department export licenses during most of 1982 to ship $175 million worth of rotors, nozzles, and stator blades), the three European firms would have to had found alternatives to these essential components. Without the proper rotors and blades, the 25 MW gas-driven turbines are useless. The compressor stations need turbines to push the gas through the pipeline. Alternative European turbine suppliers could have been found, but design changes would have been necessary. Had that route been chosen, the companies and governments involved would have violated the January 11, 1982, North Atlantic Council declaration pledging each ally not to undercut the others' sanctions against Poland and the Soviet Union.

Only state-controlled Alsthom-Atlantique of France could have supplied the denied GE parts, but the company was already participating in the pipeline project (Alsthom has a contract to supply forty spare rotor sets beginning in 1984) and had only one factory producing turbine components. The plant was working at full capacity, and orders were backlogged for at least several years. A spokesman for Alsthom noted the "obvious political risks" involved in accepting additional Soviet orders given the uncertain nature of future East-West relations.[5] Alsthom is wary of gearing up another production line in light of the French government's declaration that the contract would be abrogated should a Soviet invasion of Poland commence.

Additionally, the product belongs to GE, and violating their contract status with GE by selling the turbine components might have jeopardized Alsthom's long-term relationship with its U.S. licenser. The French government's intervention in behalf of Alsthom, however, signaled President Mitterrand's willingness to confront the Reagan administration's export-control policy. Alsthom was thus bolstered by French legislation insisting that all Franco-Soviet contracts for 1982 would have to be honored. Significantly, President Mitterrand did not move further by granting Alsthom new subsidies to begin an additional production line for new turbine and/or rotor set construction.

GE exported enough rotor sets for twenty-three turbines prior to the imposition of U.S. sanctions, but the Reagan administration had demanded that GE's manufacturing associates not use those components. A major test of U.S. export-control law might have occurred if the U.S. government decided to apply the export controls, which would have made it illegal for GE's European licensees to utilize the American parts in their Soviet-bound turbines. The decision to apply export control rules following martial law in Poland was postponed after harsh reaction was received from many domestic and allied quarters, including the U.S. Chamber of Commerce, which asked the president in March 1982 not to declare economic warfare against U.S. allies. With twenty-three compressors in operation, about 70 percent of the designed throughput capacity could be reached, but there would have been little room for operations failure because there would have been no reserve turbines initially.

Alternative suppliers, such as Rolls Royce of Great Britain, Brown, Boveri of the FRG, or Sulzer of Switzerland, might not have been able to provide similar equipment in the time frame put forth. Utilizing Rolls Royce blades and rotors would have required the entire turbine to be redesigned, which would have eliminated AEG-Kanis from participation. The Rolls Royce RB-211 aircraft turbine would have been a more-efficient machine but would have required much greater maintenance and attention, clearly not in the interest of the poorly equipped and organized Soviet technician crews. It was improbable in any event that Prime Minister Margaret Thatcher would have granted Rolls Royce an export license, despite her determination to see John Brown & Company's contract fulfilled.

In March 1982, the Buckley mission to Western Europe visited NATO capitals ostensibly to dissuade participating allies from following through on their contracts. Led by James L. Buckley, then the under secretary of state for security assistance, science and technology, the mission reportedly focused not on the pipeline—a lost cause as far as former Secretary of State Alexander M. Haig, Jr., and former Assistant Secretary of State for Economic and Business Affairs Robert Hormats were concerned—but rather on a common allied program to restrict future export credits to Soviet bloc nations.

At the June 1982 Versailles Big Seven economic summit, President Reagan did not attempt to reverse European participation in the pipeline project, as he did at the Ottawa Summit in 1981. Instead the American delegation received a unified European pledge to proceed with caution and to exercise "commercial prudence" in extending credits and conducting trade with the Soviet bloc. Each state, however, was to remain free to determine thresholds of imprudence or incaution. It was this final caveat—evidenced through European refusal to eradicate the policy of interest-rate subsidization in trade with the CMEA, as well as the French disavowal of the U.S interpretation of the Versaille accord—that in large part contributed to President Reagan's June 18, 1982, decision to broaden the scope of the December 1981 export controls.

American Sanctions, Round Two

On June 18, 1982, the president announced the extension of the ban on U.S. participation in the pipeline project.[6] The proximate cause was lack of movement toward reconciliation in Poland. In December 1981, export controls were enacted against the USSR in retaliation for assumed Soviet complicity in the martial-law decision of December 13. A six-month review period was simultaneously announced in order to compel Soviet and Polish authorities to end martial law quickly and resume dialogue between the state, the church, and the Solidarity labor movement.

Under the second round of U.S. sanctions, the transfer of U.S.-licensed oil and gas equipment and technology to the Soviet Union was prohibited.[7] The amended export controls particularly affected General Electric's manufacturing associates, as well as Dallas-based Dresser Industries' subsidiary (Dresser France S.A.). Both companies held substantial turbine and compressor contracts, respectively, for the Siberian export pipeline.

Rather than develop competing 25 MW turbine and turbine-component technologies for natural-gas-pipeline compressor stations, corporate decisions were taken years ago in the relevant European industries to rely instead upon GE's rotor sets. The high-speed rotor, licensed by the U.S. Department of Commerce, is widely considered the most-reliable gas-turbine equipment, requiring maintenance once every 20,000 hours. Contrasted with the current Soviet 10 MW turbine, which requires maintenance once every 800 hours, the GE-designed turbines are a model of efficiency and thus highly desired. GE then feared that the expanded export-controls decision would foster a direct challenge to its worldwide turbine market share, as the capability to design 25 MW turbines independent of GE's proprietary technology is no longer in doubt.

President Reagan, believing that the economics of the pipeline would worsen should the project be sufficiently delayed, therefore attempted to raise the financial costs of the project in an effort to persuade U.S. allies in Europe to rethink their participation. In addition, the White House believed that the imposition of broad export controls affecting both subsidiaries of U.S. firms as well as manufacturing associates in Europe would impel those affected businesses (and by extension, their respective governments) to pressure Moscow to ease or lift martial law in Poland.

Allied reaction to the administration's new policy, however, was uniformly hostile. Prime Minister Margaret Thatcher of Great Britain ordered the Ministry of Trade to prepare rules by which British companies (including U.S. subsidiaries) would be forced to disregard the U.S. export-control laws should Parliament invoke the 1980 Protection of Trading Interests Act. Given active U.S. support for Great Britain during the British-Argentine war over the Falkland Islands, at substantial cost to U.S. diplomacy in Latin America, many officials in the Reagan administration, who counted on Prime Minister Thatcher for support in Europe, were greatly dismayed.

The French government was the first ally to defy the Reagan ban legally by issuing an administrative decree in July 1982 insisting that all Franco-Soviet contracts for 1982 be honored. West Germany, Italy, and Great Britain quickly closed ranks behind the French government and encouraged U.S. subsidiaries and nationally chartered companies to defy the extended export controls. President Mitterrand was spared the decision of granting Alsthom-Atlantique additional subsidies to begin a new turbine production line to cover the remaining fifty-seven 25 MW turbines.[8] Finally, the Japanese threatened to file a formal protest, an indication of extreme displeasure, because the consortium of Japanese oil companies managing the Soviet-Japanese Sakhalin Island Oil Project was prevented from leasing U.S.-licensed well-logging equipment used in offshore drilling in the Sea of Okhotsk.

Remaining options for turbine and compressor replacement ensured that the pipeline's construction would not have been significantly delayed. Assuming that the Rolls Royce turbine would have been rejected by the construction managers or disallowed by the British government, several alternatives would have been available for the affected parties.

The policy that was chosen consisted of Moscow's encouragement of West European companies to violate the American export controls to fulfill as much of their contracts as possible. Inducement along these lines was aided by a clause conferring upon Moscow the right to penalize monetarily participating companies that violate their contracts. It is estimated that the penalty could be as much as 5 percent of the value of the entire contract.

The European Community (EC) delivered a diplomatic note and legal comments to the U.S. Departments of State and Commerce on August 12, 1982, just a few days prior to the expiration of the Commerce Department's interim rule period. The interim rule period refers to the period of time in the extended export-controls decision covering reexports to the USSR, between June 22 and August 21, 1982, in which notes and comments can be received in reaction to a new rule or regulation before such a rule becomes permanent. It is instructive to examine the language of the EC note in reference to the question of future technology flows:

> One inevitable consequence would be to call in question the usefulness of technological links between European and American firms, if contracts could be nullified at any time by decision of the U.S. administration. Another consequence to be feared is that the claim of U.S. jurisdiction accompanying U.S. investment will create a resistance abroad to the flow of U.S. investment.[9]

Development of a commercially competitive 25 MW European turbine model, based on an independent (non-GE) design, might still be undertaken as a result of the sanctions. The time frame necessary for research, development, and production of such turbines, variously given as between two and five years, is less urgent when one considers that gas deliveries, scheduled to begin in late 1984, will build slowly and reach planned capacity (now significantly reduced pending Italian participation) only by the late 1980s. Therefore a European turbine or perhaps a Soviet-European joint-venture turbine project is a possibility despite the Reagan administration's discontinuation of its expanded export-controls decision against U.S. allies in Europe.

Another option lent credence by Soviet pronouncements is Moscow's assertion that the entire compressor station, including the 25 MW gas turbine, can be built in the USSR without Western assistance.[10] Prototype 16 MW and 25 MW turbines have already been domestically manufactured, but the capacity to mass produce a reliable gas-driven 25 MW turbine (two have been produced to date) by the mid-1980s must surely be questioned.

Soviet threats to cut the West European contractors and subcontractors out of the compressor construction must be viewed with considerable skepticism, given that the European commitment to the pipeline project rests in large part on the employment and profits generated by equipment sales, in which billions of dollars in large-diameter steel pipe and compressor-station exports comprise the bulk of projected earnings. The Soviet announcement must therefore be treated as an effort to pressure the NATO allies into challenging the Reagan ban on energy-technology trade with the Soviet bloc while it lasted. It is doubtful that such a strategy would prove effective, at least in the near term. It is apparent, however, that the technological and manufacturing capability within Europe and Japan to produce 25 MW turbines comparable to GE's product could have been used if necessary.

Alternatively, it was suggested that Moscow utilize two smaller turbines in place of the single 25 MW GE turbine; but such an alternative would have required greater maintenance and operations costs; moreover there is a lack of skilled personnel. The two-turbine option is technically feasible, however, and was presumed to be under active consideration. Compressor engines powered by electric or diesel power, replacing the turbine as generator, seemed impractical because of the failure to install adequate electricity capacity along the proposed route. Gas-driven turbines are therefore the most-desirable option inasmuch as they utilize the compressed natural gas as a source of power.

American export controls and European defiance of those controls guaranteed an escalation of tension between the postwar allies and trading partners. Whether the imbroglio over the Siberian pipeline is merely symptomatic of a deteriorating alliance or whether it simply represents a deeply rooted philosophical difference concerning the merits of East-West trade is unclear at this juncture. In my view, the pipeline dispute cannot by itself fracture the set of common interests and political traditions that bind together the Western alliance. Rather than place additional strain on an increasingly troubled partnership, however, the United States, as alliance leader, must seek to lower rather than raise the level of intra-allied confrontation. It is therefore important to inquire whether the broadened export controls served to "further significantly the foreign policy of the United States."[11]

Energy-Export Controls: Alliance Implications

Diplomatic efforts aimed at promoting reconciliation in Poland, both with NATO allies and through unilateral measures, have thus far proved unsuccessful. The extraterritorial controls apparently offered President Reagan a final possibility to influence allied participation, which in turn was intended to damage Soviet economic interests at home and in Eastern Europe.

Were U.S. foreign-policy goals significantly furthered by the June 18 decision? The criteria listed in section 6 of the Export Administration Act of 1979 enable one to assess the impact of foreign-policy controls, an export-control category separate from national-security controls in its lack of technical precision and in its broad language concerning an adversary's acquisition of U.S. products or technology deemed militarily significant.[12] The major criteria that must be satisfied prior to the imposition of foreign-policy controls are:

The probability that U.S. controls will achieve the intended foreign-policy objective.

The reactions of other countries "to the imposition or expansion" of U.S. controls.

The effects of the controls on U.S. export competitiveness, on the U.S.'s international economic position, on the credibility of the United States as a reliable supplier of goods and technology, and on individual companies affected by such controls.

The ability to enforce controls effectively, as well as the foreign-policy consequences of not imposing such controls.[13]

The only condition fulfilled by the imposition of the extended oil and gas controls was the clause relating to the foreign-policy consequences of not imposing controls. By not imposing such controls, U.S. foreign policy would have undermined the cause of Polish reconciliation, in large part because the United States would have abdicated its role as leader of an alliance outraged by Soviet-Polish suppression of popular dissent.

The remaining criteria could not have been satisfied. The proscribed goods and technology could be acquired abroad in a relatively short period of time, independent of U.S. license. U.S. blocking actions could have delayed the project by approximately two years, but a two-year delay measured against a twenty-five-year gas-supply contract is clearly negligible, particularly striking when one considers the phased-in nature of the gas-delivery schedules to Western Europe.

The expanded oil and gas controls further undermine U.S. credibility as a reliable supplier of goods and technology, which can only undermine U.S. export competitiveness. Unreliable suppliers in turn impel foreign importers of U.S.-licensed designs to turn elsewhere or to develop their own technologies. Individual companies were hurt not only in the immediate circumstances relating to the pipeline construction but possibly in the long run as well because of the potential emergence of new competitors in what is often a small and specialized market (such as GE's domination of the gas-turbine market).

Finally, the enforcement of controls extends only to U.S.-licensed goods and technology, not to goods produced abroad through independent design, such as pipe layers or earth movers. The placement of Creusot-Loire and Dresser-France on a thirty-day temporary denial list in late August 1982 prohibited those two companies from receiving any U.S.-origin exports but cannot prevent these firms from importing the required blacklisted items from elsewhere or eventually developing the necessary parts or services themselves. Enforcement of export controls can rarely, if ever, prevent similar technology or products from being devised and diffused either in the OECD or in the CMEA.

It was plausible that Soviet diversion of 10 MW turbines for the export line's compressor stations could have set back the construction progress of the additional five domestic natural-gas pipelines, vital for expanded gas-utilization plans. The manufacture of 10 MW turbines in the USSR would not have proven to be a major bottleneck; in fact, production of additional turbines could well have fit into the typical Soviet construction schedule given the usual time lag between the laying down of pipe and the installation of compressor stations.

The furor in Europe and the inability of the United States to cause any substantial delay in either the pipeline's contruction or in the gas deliveries to Western Europe created the aura of an ineffectual U.S. foreign policy. In early November 1982, the president withdrew the export controls, without mention of Poland, and announced in their place a common allied approach to East-West trade to which the French promptly refused accession. The new accords, requiring further negotiation and refinement, feature common policies toward export credit restraint, interest-rate subsidies, energy alternatives in Western Europe, and tighter controls in the transfer of advanced technology from West to East. The rifts between the transatlantic allies arising from the Reagan administration's expanded export controls could well have created far greater security problems for the North Atlantic community than would the Soviet pipeline to Western Europe. The dissolution of mutual trust between allies who still need one another to deter Soviet military action in Europe must be countered and the process reversed. Proliferation of protectionist trade sentiment will exacerbate the political and military difficulties encountered since the December 1979 NATO decision to deploy intermediate nuclear forces while pursuing parallel arms-control negotiations with the Soviet Union.

In this context, key allied government elites, who more often than not defend U.S.-sponsored policies in European capitals, particularly on such explosive issues as long-range theater nuclear-force modernization, maintenance of the nuclear-response option to conventional Soviet attack, or the commitment to achieve real increases in annual defense expenditures, can be expected to distance themselves from overtly pro-American positions when public discontent with the United States grows. A host of equally, if not more, important security interests would have been jeopardized on behalf of an issue that was widely regarded as a lost cause.

In addition, U.S. credibility as a sincere economic summit partner is cast into doubt because coordinated policies (even least-common-denominator policies) will be perceived as short term in nature. Barely two weeks had passed when President Reagan reversed the Versailles summit bargain through the imposition of the extended sanctions. The timing of the president's announcement proved politically embarrassing for those governments dedicated to the principles of the annual economic summit process: that the major OECD partners should seek common solutions to major international economic problems based on goodwill, fair play, and mutual trust.

European Attitudes

The perceptions of European elites are by no means uniform, but it is clear that a solid majority of informed opinion in Western Europe supports expanded East-West trade. The West German government and German industry have assumed a major role in defending the project, perhaps because the United States has leveled the lion's share of criticism at the Federal Republic as the largest recipient of the new Soviet gas and as the largest financial participant.

There are four important issues for Western Europe in regard to the Siberian pipeline: security of energy supply, fuel-use shift toward greater natural-gas utilization, alleviation of unemployment and recession, and the preservation of European détente. These concerns, extremely urgent politically, have become entwined in the North Atlantic debate over the merits of the proposed pipeline.

Security of supply has come to imply diversification away from unstable Middle East and North African oil-producing states. NATO-Europe imports

about 45 percent of its oil, most of which (between 60 and 70 percent) origi-
nates in the Persian Gulf. Western Europe has observed with dismay the
changing terms of commercial access to oil supplies, noting that national oil
companies outside the OECD owned 55 percent of their crude oil by 1981,
up from 6 percent just a decade before. Producing states have doubled their
share of refined-product sales (from 9 to 18 percent in the same period), an
alarming prospect to a European refinery industry that increasingly sees
mass bankruptcy just over the horizon.[14]

Western Europe further questions the Reagan administration's commitment to the International Energy Agency (IEA) and fears that the free-market
approach to energy emergencies will mitigate the effective functioning of the
IEA's emergency oil-sharing program. In addition, price disagreements with
Algeria over the cost of high-quality crude oil and natural gas, continued
uncertainties concerning the efficaciousness of U.S. policy in the Arab-
Israeli dispute, and regional sociopolitical dynamics threatening to broaden
the scope of the Iran-Iraq war or topple oil regimes friendly to the West
have combined to persuade Western Europe that backing out oil where applicable and Persian Gulf oil in particular would make for prudent policy.

Much of OECD-Europe has decided that natural-gas substitution (for
both oil and nuclear, especially in Austria and perhaps the FRG) is the
most-economical and politically acceptable alternative to oil. In this context, reliance on the USSR for additional natural-gas imports allows a fairly
rapid oil back-out program because the Soviet gas deposits seem relatively
proximate, less expensive to develop and transport than other alternatives,
and fit in readily with the extant European gas network.

Increasing natural-gas consumption proved worrisome to industrial and
government analysts, who foresaw a burgeoning gap between domestic and
imported gas supply and growing demand. They then argued that reliance
on Soviet gas would constitute but one import source. Algeria, Libya, Nigeria, Ghana, Cameroon, the Netherlands (until the early 1990s), and Norway could be enlisted or persuaded to supply liquefied natural gas (LNG) or
conventional pipeline gas to supplement the new Soviet imports. Recently
Ruhrgas of the FRG and Gaz de France have approached Canadian energy
companies with joint-venture proposals to develop LNG facilities in the
Canadian Arctic and export the LNG to the FRG and France. With European demand for imported natural gas expected to double or triple in the
next twenty years, several NATO allies firmly believe that they will be forced
to rely on a variety of import sources, not only the USSR.

Third, unemployment and recession are at their worst levels in over
twenty-five years. In the FRG, not since January 1956 has the unemployment rate exceeded 8.2 percent (just under 2 million people). French unemployment surpassed the 2 million mark in early 1982, about 8.5 percent of
the work force. As 1981 drew to a close, it was evident that the governing

coalitions in the FRG and France needed the jobs creation generated by the pipeline and compressor sales. There were no other comparable export markets for large-diameter pipe or compressor turbines.

Through 1984-1985, the project should add 20,000 to 25,000 jobs in the FRG and about half that figure or slightly more in France. In the FRG, where some 220,000 jobs are directly and indirectly dependent upon East-West trade, the additions to the labor force will affect the overall German unemployment rate only marginally. Politically, however, those new jobs are seen as government-sponsored movement on the economic front because the governments involved have provided loan guarantees to the financial-industrial packages negotiated with Moscow.

Both former Chancellor Schmidt and President Mitterrand have complained about high American interest rates, which they believe have worsened Europe's economic downturn and, ironically, coalesced otherwise neutral opinion in favor of any project that contributes to economic growth. The lack of a concrete American counterproposal or set of proposals that could compete not only in terms of price but, equally important, in European jobs creation, doomed the series of U.S. initiatives to halt the pipeline.

In this regard, the U.S. offer to expand steam-coal deliveries and engage in greater nuclear-power cooperation fell far short in both timing and volume of a realistic alternative to Soviet gas. The expansion of U.S. steam-coal exports is dependent upon deep-water port expansion and construction on the East Coast. The Reagan administration deleted funds for these and related purposes, and the Congress cannot be expected to move very quickly either. Nuclear power is unpopular in large segments of European societies and faces long legal delays and lead-time problems. Both U.S. coal and more nuclear power, however, do not match the employment benefits engendered by the Siberian pipeline, nor do they match the prospect of renewed profits for the FRG's largest electrical and pipe-making concerns. The logic of accusing Western Europe of trading with the enemy is lost upon allied industrial and governmental officials, who point to continued U.S. exports of grain to the Soviet Union.

Heightened concern with economic pressures matched the political requirements to strengthen détente, for the impulse to be perceived as a peacemaker fits in neatly with increased jobs and profits stemming from greater East-West trade. Trade, not isolation and confrontation, is the hallmark of the West German policy of Ostpolitik, realized by Chancellor Brandt through German-Soviet and inter-German treaty arrangements in 1969 and by 1982 a sine qua non of FRG foreign policy.

Through Ostpolitik and Soviet-West European détente has come a loosening of the tight controls previously imposed on inter-German contacts. The expansion of East-West trade reinforces cross-bloc interdependence, which, it is theorized, will modify Soviet behavior inside the CMEA and in turn will make Soviet action more accountable to Western economic decisions. Thus, European détente benefits both Eastern Europe and the West. According to this view, aggressive or hostile policies will be mitigated by Soviet dependence on Western credit and technology.

The French government under François Mitterrand does not necessarily subscribe to the moderation-through-trade theory. Rather they have chosen to debate the pipeline's merits primarily on economic grounds. Most governments in Europe, however, were in agreement that NATO sanctions stemming from Soviet involvement in the Polish crackdown should have extended only to new contracts and credit negotiations, that Europe badly needs the jobs and the natural gas, and that, by and large, East-West trade remains a viable mechanism for the promotion of détente and mutual trust.

The U.S. Perspective

In 1979 and 1980, the Carter administration was faced with an old theoretical dilemma: would greater activity in East-West trade moderate Soviet foreign policy and strengthen détente, or would it merely provide Moscow with a new and expanded stream of hard-currency revenue in which the military sector would continue to receive a large allotment (and could then offer the Politburo more and varied military options to settle international disputes)? The Soviet invasion of Afghanistan at the close of 1979 prevented this issue from being fully explored, for domestic political reaction to the Soviet intervention, not strategic-economic analysis, determined the American response. Sanctions were imposed, and advanced-technology transfers were denied export licenses.

President Carter did not actively oppose energy-technology trade with the Soviet Union. During his administration, Dresser Industries sold a drill-bit turnkey factory, which could serve to improve the Soviet oil industry's prospects for recovery of deep oil. During the Nixon administration, the North Star LNG project utilizing gas from Yakutia was proposed but floundered on the economic unattractiveness of the deal. After Angola, large Soviet-American energy ventures became little more than abstract economic exercises.

With Afghanistan still occupied by Soviet troops and Poland's Solidarity movement suppressed by military force, President Reagan asked the NATO allies and Japan to withdraw their commitments to supply material for the pipeline. On January 11, 1982, the NATO allies pledged that each would refrain from undercutting another's sanctions. At the January 19-20, 1982, CoCom meeting (the Coordinating Committee on Multilateral Export Controls), the U.S. government clarified its position.

The United States fears European overreliance on Soviet gas imports, which will range from between 15 and 30 percent of total gas consumption for four of the major participants (see table 4-3). While the total energy-consumption dependence on the USSR will be about 5 to 6 percent in the FRG and France, certain regions and industrial sectors will be highly dependent upon Soviet gas. Bavaria, the heart of the German chemical, petrochemical, and automotive industries, today receives 80 to 90 percent of its gas consumption from the Soviet Union. The Saar and the Rhineland use Soviet gas for about half their total consumption.[15] Other industrial centers in the FRG in all probability would begin taking Soviet gas, as would many residential units.

Moreover, the United States fears that gas-storage facilities, which are very expensive and difficult to maintain, will not receive adequate attention. Gas consumption in the residential and commercial sector has grown, as has natural gas in OECD-Europe's energy mix. The flexibility required to switch quickly out of gas is inadequate in the residential-commercial sector and leaves many home owners and businesses vulnerable to a supply curtailment.

Most importantly, the United States sees heightened Soviet leverage resulting from the project. The impetus not to oppose Soviet political initiatives in times of tension or crisis is feared, bolstered by an industrial-financial lobby with an active stake in East-West trade and therefore détente, however imbalanced or unreciprocal. Price ratcheting in a tight market would be furthered by East-West crises as well, assuming that any gas would be exported in a severe emergency. Alliance cohesion and even symbolic Western gestures could prove increasingly difficult to muster.

The U.S. Defense Department in particular has warned of the dangers of strengthened Soviet leverage in Western Europe, and additionally of the hard-currency earnings the Soviet Union will be capable of earning: $7.6 billion per year at the initial design capacity.[16] If the price of competitive fuels in the European market of the late 1980s and early 1990s increases in

Table 4-3
European Reliance on Soviet Natural-Gas Imports as a Share of Total Gas Consumption
(percent)

	1980	*1990[a]*
West Germany	18-20	25-30
France	10	25-30
Italy	20-22	22-25
Austria	55	65
Belgium	0	15-20

[a]Assumes that pipeline reaches full capacity of 40 bcm.

real terms, then the Soviets will earn still more hard currency. The Reagan administration has warned of the consequences that follow from a policy of energy trade with the Soviet Union: such trade allows Moscow to avoid serious economic reform and, in effect, provides an indirect subsidy for the continuation of outmoded and inefficient production practices. The political leadership, then, is not forced to divert scarce resources away from the military sector and toward energy projects or consumer-oriented light industries. Grain and technology can be imported, and Soviet defense spending can continue at a steady pace.

The U.S. government would like to see European exploration and development focused on the North Sea, where a recent study commissioned by the Department of Defense forecasts a doubling of existing reserves by 1985 to 380 tcf (10.76 tcm). Equipment orders from the new investment would satisfy European demands for pipeline-related business while providing a politically secure source of natural gas for continental Europe.[17]

Implications

If the additional exports of Soviet natural gas are delivered as envisaged by the close of 1981 (table 4-1), West European dependence on Soviet natural-gas imports will grow by a substantial margin (see table 4-3).

Natural-gas consumption in the FRG, France, and Italy is 17 percent, 12 percent, and 17 percent, respectively, of total primary energy consumption. These percentages have been steadily growing since 1975 and will continue to rise through 2000.[18] Demand dropped by 4 percent between 1980 and 1981, but projections of a gap between gas supply and demand increasing throughout the 1990s still hold as the Netherlands' Groningen field peaks and declines and as other major continental gas fields in Germany and France dry up. Diversification out of high-priced oil within OECD-Europe leaves natural gas as the most-desirable alternative, a development compounded by future concern over the stability of Middle East and, in particular, Persian Gulf oil-producing regimes.

Further, imports of natural gas comprise the bulk of gas consumption in the energy mix of the major participants, assuming for uncertainty's sake that Italy decides to follow through on its contract (table 4-4). In addition to the USSR, the Netherlands, Algeria, Libya, and Norway supply gas to inland Western Europe.

The final distribution of gas consumption must be discussed as well, for the sectoral breakdown enables one to pinpoint the likely political and economic effects in the event of a supply curtailment (table 4-5).

The residential and commercial sector does not have the same short-run flexibility to switch between oil and gas should a disruption occur. Table 4-5

Table 4-4
Approximate Shares of Imports in Natural-Gas Consumption
(percent)

West Germany	67
France	70
Italy	55
Austria	64

Source: Conversations with U.S. government and European embassy officials.

shows that the high level of gas use in Italian industry and in the French and German residential-commercial sectors (coupled with the very high share of imports in total consumption) renders all three nations subject to significant economic and political problems in the event of supply bottlenecks or cut-offs. Both West Germany and France plan to increase the number of inter-ruptible contracts with industrial consumers as a security measure, a decision that could leave many industries exposed in a combined oil-and-gas shortfall.

Although the economic impact of a Soviet gas curtailment would be adverse—primarily depending on gas-storage programs, substitutability, and surge capacity—the political leverage gained by Soviet gas penetration is potentially more far-reaching. In a tightening fuels market, for example, a significant supply disruption would leave many areas in the FRG, France, and Italy without heat or power. Moscow could pressure one of these governments on an important policy dispute, but all would suffer (the Soviets could point to "technical difficulties" as they have in the past with Western

Table 4-5
End-Use Distribution of Natural Gas, 1979
(percent)

	Industry	Residential-Commercial	Utility
Sector's share of gas market			
West Germany	34	35	31
France	44	47	8
Italy	50	37	13
Sectoral dependence on gas			
West Germany	21	19	18
France	15	18	2
Italy	24	27	6

Source: Boyce I. Greer, "Soviet Natural Gas Exports and West European Security: The Yamburg Natural Gas Pipeline" (unpublished manuscript, Harvard University, June 23, 1981), p. 15.

Europe); governments not involved with the dispute in turn would pressure the hold-out to accommodate Soviet interests, thus fracturing alliance cohesion. The threat of a disruption, after the primary Soviet natural-gas pipeline network is largely completed between northwest Siberia and the western provinces, would be just as effective. The USSR could obtain spare parts from many sources unless a common West European "spare-parts" strategy is worked out in advance, an unlikely prospect under present conditions. Leverage therefore will be imbalanced in favor of the energy supplier, not the energy purchaser.

The Europeans have noted that surge-capacity potential exists in the Netherlands and that gas-stockpiling programs are actively underway in the International Energy Agency (IEA), the European Economic Community (EEC), the FRG, and Italy. In addition, about 75 percent of West German gas utilities can switch quickly to oil.[19] Each of these points, however, must be considered superficial in light of the realities of practical politics and economic decision making. Dutch surge capacity as a European strategic reserve should be viewed in the context of declining Dutch reserves. Southern North Sea gas potential is limited, with Denmark, the Netherlands, and the FRG together sharing only 5 percent of North Sea proven oil and gas reserves.[20] Dutch demand is scheduled to rise steadily, and it therefore can be expected that excess or new capacity will be slated for the Dutch market.

There is much better gas potential in the Norwegian sector north of 62° North latitude, but the difficulties and expense associated with exploration and development could well delay the necessary investment required to make the northern Norwegian North Sea a surplus or supplemental gas supplier by the early 1990s, especially if European gas demand increases at a slower pace than envisaged in 1979 and 1980. In this regard, continental Europe may be locking itself into greater reliance on Soviet gas than expected. Much of the infrastructure will be laid down in the USSR. The gas is plentiful, and therefore large Western investment in the North Sea could be considered increasingly uneconomic relative to reliance upon northwest Siberia.

Will aggressive gas-stockpile programs be undertaken in the FRG, France, and Italy? In these three countries, storage capacity at present totals 20.2 bcm, about thirty-five days of 1981 gas consumption, broken down as follows: Italy, 9.4 bcm; France, 7.3 bcm; FRG, 3.5 bcm.[21] As inland gas consumption increases, the strategic reserves will have to be expanded accordingly. Storage capacity today represents about 3-4 percent of annual German gas consumption and the plans to treble existing capacity will represent 9 percent of projected 1990 consumption. Just under half of 1990 German gas consumption, however, will be imported, whereas only one-third of present consumption is imported. Any projected gains from gas stockpile growth will thus be balanced by a greater percentage of imports.

With budgetary constraints growing worse rather than improving, expensive gas-storage capacity may be among the first items to be eliminated or reduced under tight economic conditions. The IEA's emphasis is oil stocks, and it has proven difficult enough to convince many member-states to undertake adequate oil-emergency preparedness efforts. Coordination of response in an oil and/or gas emergency would probably strain the existing mechanisms for coping with disruption. Similarly, utilities in the FRG that are dual capable (readily switched between oil and gas) may not find the requisite oil needed or may locate the proper product mix but at exorbitant prices in an emergency.

LNG potential in West Africa and along the Persian Gulf littoral may fall subject to similar investment shortfalls. The Bonny LNG project in Nigeria has been cancelled, with few hopes that Nigerian LNG will reach Western Europe prior to 1990. The costs involved with LNG transport, a major impediment in addition to costly gas-gathering and -processing facilities, will remain prohibitive unless many projects currently in trouble (including West and North African pipeline-gas proposals traversing the Sahara) are built in a reasonable time frame. If the market for imported gas in Europe is perceived as impenetrable as a result of the Soviet price advantage, these North-South energy projects in natural-gas development will be scrapped or scaled back. The OECD thus loses an opportunity to further economic cooperation and development programs that would tap developing-country energy resources and assist in their modernization process.

Finally, U.S. steam-coal exports to Western Europe will continue their growth but will not be as cost- or environmentally competitive with Soviet natural gas. Burning coal under boilers for utility purposes and in industrial furnaces will undoubtedly grow, but the United States will have to move now in order to secure a sizable place for U.S. coal in European economies because decisions to burn gas instead of coal are based on economic availabilities and only secondarily (if at all) on security grounds. Hence Soviet or other imported natural gas, not coal (or at least not American coal), may be increasingly viewed as the preferred alternative to OPEC oil.

What are the policy implications of the dilemmas posed by the Siberian pipeline project? What Moscow gains, and the effects of those gains on the Western alliance system, are discussed next.

Hard Currency

Estimates of Soviet hard-currency earnings vary from a low of $5 billion to $6 billion for the first few years of the amortization period to $15 billion to $20 billion as full capacity is reached and debts are paid off. Many necessary imports (in particular energy technologies and wheat) will be purchased. Economic growth will be high enough so that the extant subsidy and energy-supply program to Eastern Europe can be maintained or improved. The gas-pipeline network west of the Urals will be greatly expanded close to schedule and domestic energy programs significantly improved. Military spending and the stress on heavy industries will not have to be cut. While it cannot be assumed that military expenditures would otherwise be reduced without the pipeline earnings, the lack of hard currency, the bloc's economic setbacks, and the greater difficulties involved in deeper resource extraction and long-distance transport could plausibly have forced a reluctant USSR to scale back some defense efforts. In this regard, the mid-1980s cannot be thought of as similar to past periods of economic difficulties. The Soviet bloc has experienced expanding growth rates since the early postwar years and recently has come to rely on Western loans and trade. With economic growth abruptly slowing and absolute factor supply dwindling, the USSR in particular will be forced (in the absence of improvements in efficiency) to reallocate resources in order to retain hard-currency earnings.

Improving efficiency through gains in industrial productivity will be a long and arduous process, one in which it is in the West's interest to promote if it channels Soviet efforts toward nonthreatening industrial (as against ever-growing military) competition. The disproportionately high investment levels in Soviet defense-related sectors suggest that the military would gain little in the way of future spin-offs from energy or light industry innovations.

In turn, the prospect of economic crises could compel a hard-pressed leadership to redirect more investment into hard-currency natural-resource export projects and consumer-oriented industries. Economic and social discontent would then be easier to contain in Eastern Europe. The successful completion of the pipeline on current terms, however, would reduce future Western reform pressures to ineffective posturing.

The U.S. government argues further that Soviet dependence on U.S. wheat shipments drains their financial reserves and could well worsen as Soviet agricultural problems multiply. European analysts respond that if the United States were intent on seeing the pipeline cancelled, President Reagan would first have had to reimpose President Carter's post-Afghanistan grain embargo, lifted in April 1981. While the punitive value of a reimposed grain embargo may be far less than the symbolic import, political realities are such that many Europeans perceive the U.S. economy suffering no penalty in lost trade opportunities, while a more trade-dependent Europe bears the brunt of cancelled East-West projects. Former Chancellor Schmidt of the FRG has suggested, with some degree of cynicism, that the pipeline project is necessary for Moscow to continue earning hard currency in order to import U.S. grain.

In fact, over 80 percent of Soviet grain imports, estimated at over 40 million tons for 1982, will come from non-U.S. sources, particularly Argentina, Canada, and the EEC. Further, while measurement problems make absolute determinations of import effectiveness an uncertain task, a general argument can be made that steel pipe is a more-important strategic commodity than grain in the Soviet context. The agricultural sector, unlike the energy sector, suffers from both environmental and organizational difficulties. The richness of the West Siberian oil and gas provinces, however, far surpasses in quality the best arable soil. In short, regardless of grain-import levels or bureaucratic reorganizations, Soviet agricultural production and distribution appears fated to perform poorly. The same cannot be said of energy. Imports of pipe and compressors will greatly improve the hard-currency-earning energy sector (particularly in natural-gas development) while contributing to domestic logistical and strategic capabilities. Without significant pipe and compressor imports, the domestic-gas-expansion program would encounter delays. Much effort and reallocation of resources would have been required to fulfill the contracted production schedules for the export line, which would undoubtedly have slowed the progress of the remaining five major gas-pipeline projects to 1985.

Allied Disunity

The intra-alliance dispute over the pipeline should serve to remind the West that there is an equally important economic component to strategic problems. Soviet foreign policy places the splintering of the NATO system at or near the top of desirable objectives and as such seeks to isolate Western Europe from the United States.

The outcry in European public opinion against the modernization of NATO's long-range theater nuclear forces in the autumn of 1981 parallels the fervent support the pipeline project has received. The Siberian pipeline represents the economic counterpart to the security component, which together characterize the anxious nature of the transatlantic rift. It is interesting to note that while the European allied leaders agree that Moscow is responsible for Poland's martial-law decision, their participation in the pipeline was not cancelled despite warnings following Afghanistan that détente could not survive such a blow within Europe. Criticism was deflected through reference to Yalta. European détente has survived Poland, while historians note that Chancellor Brandt's version of Ostpolitik was launched less than a year after Soviet-led Warsaw Pact units crushed the Prague Spring in Czechoslovakia in 1968.

The strategic implications of a perpetually divided alliance are far-reaching and, in the case of the Siberian pipeline, extend beyond mere logistic or economic asymmetries. From an alliance perspective, it is more worrisome that a unified and consistent NATO grand strategy (encompassing

East-West trade and credit issues) cannot reach consensus than it is to note that over 90 percent of Bavaria has become dependent on Soviet gas imports. Despite CoCom's decision in 1982 to tighten their strategic-goods list, allied councils are still divided over fundamental questions pertaining to NATO's raison d'être: Soviet policy in Europe and long-term Soviet intentions.

U.S. options are limited; the pipeline can and will be built without U.S. participation. As a symbol of détente in a time of heightened concern over the imminence of a new round in nuclear-weapons acquisitions and deployments, the Siberian pipeline has widespread support across the European political spectrum, and active U.S. efforts to sabotage the deal have proven counterproductive.

When the project was first proposed, a variety of energy alternatives to Soviet gas might have been successfully offered: trebling of U.S. coal exports through a crash port-expansion program; U.S. assistance in developing West African, North Sea, and Persian Gulf natural-gas resources and LNG systems looking toward Western Europe as the principal market; offers to include ailing European steel pipe producers (such as Mannesmann of the FRG) in the Alaska Natural Gas Transportation System, in addition to fostering greater transatlantic allied joint-energy ventures. Only thus could the United States have demonstrated the seriousness of American intent and the dangers believed to exist in undue reliance on East-West trade.

Henceforward, however, the following measures should be pursued:

1. Work in CoCom and through the NATO Economics Directorate to limit the extension of credits and equipment extended to the Soviet Union, to prevent other pipelines from gathering speed before they can be adequately studied and debated.
2. Advance strategic trade issues as major alliance concerns. In this regard, an alliance-wide study focusing on the pros and cons of energy-technology transfer to the Soviet bloc must be addressed.
3. Strengthen the IEA and individual country emergency-preparedness programs, especially for natural-gas storage and rapid fuel switching between oil and gas.
4. Encourage the British but especially the Norwegians to export more natural gas to Western Europe (Britain has no plans to export any gas) and to invest (with incentives to U.S. energy companies to participate) in new northerly reaches of the North Sea for a NATO surge capacity and for Norway's own export potential.
5. Encourage European diversification in natural-gas import sources, with focus on West African and Arctic LNG projects.

Adoption of these measures should mitigate most of the Reagan administration's concerns while ensuring that Western Europe does not become overly dependent on Soviet gas. East-West trade issues deserve to be placed in a special category apart from intra-alliance or North-South trade. Movement in this direction can only strengthen NATO's strategic deliberations.

Notes

1. "Pipelines Hold key to Soviet Gas Production," *Oil and Gas Journal,* June 29, 1981, p. 42. Edward Hewett has noted that during the previous Five Year Plan, the Soviets built one new large-diameter line every two years; the current plan calls for one new large-diameter line every ten months. Presentation by Edward Hewett at Seminar on Soviet Energy Prospects: Differing Perspectives, Georgetown University Center for Strategic and International Studies, February 23, 1982. The Eleventh Five Year Plan in this regard has set an ambitious schedule: for the six new West Siberian pipelines, 14 million tons of large-diameter steel pipe will be required; 20 million to 25 million tons of pipe for all pipeline requirements; and 325 compressor stations totaling 20,000 MW of capacity. Two million tons of steel pipe will have to be imported each year to meet planned commitments. Theodore Shabad, "News Notes," *Soviet Geography* (April 1982):286.

2. B.A. Rahmer, "Big Gas Deal with West Europe," *Petroleum Economist* (January 1982):13.

3. Statement of Lionel H. Olmer, Under Secretary of Commerce for International Trade, before the House Committee on Science and Technology, February 9, 1982, p. 6 (chart 1).

4. Statement of Ernest B. Johnston, Jr., Deputy Assistant Secretary of State for Economic and Business Affairs, before the House Committee on Science and Technology, February 9, 1982, p. 4.

5. "Russian Gas Pipeline Loses GE as Supplier; Only One French Company Could Fill the Gap," *Energy Daily,* January 11, 1982, p. 1.

6. Some of the material in the next two sections is excerpted from Jonathan B. Stein, "U.S. Controls and the Soviet Pipeline," *Washington Quarterly* (Fall 1982), pp. 52-59.

7. "Amendment of Oil and Gas Controls to the U.S.S.R.," *Federal Register,* June 24, 1982, p. 27250.

8. Assuming that the twenty-three previously shipped GE rotor sets will be utilized in twenty-three of the contracted turbines and that Alsthom's forty spare sets will be similarly integrated into another forty turbines, bringing the total to sixty-three, another fifty-seven turbines will be required for capacity exports. The head compressor station will use five 10 MW turbines.

9. "EC calls for Withdrawal of U.S. Pipeline Sanctions," *European Community News,* August 12, 1982, pp. 1-2.

10. Dusko Doder, "Soviets Said to Dash West's Hope for Massive Deal," *Washington Post,* June 30, 1982, p. 1; David Buchan, "Russia May Use Own Turbines on Gas Pipeline," *Financial Times,* July 30, 1982, p. 2.

11. "Amendment of Oil and Gas Controls."

12. John F. Murphy and Arthur T. Downey, "National Security, Foreign Policy and Individual Rights: The Quandary of United States Export Controls," *International and Comparative Law Quarterly* 30 (October 1981):810.

13. Section 6, Export Administration Act of 1979, P.L. 96-72, cited in ibid., p. 813.

14. Charles K. Ebinger, *The Critical Link: Energy and National Security in the 1980s* (Cambridge, Mass.: Ballinger Publishing Company, 1982), p. 123.

15. Miariam Karr and Roger W. Robinson, Jr., "Soviet Gas: Risk or Reward?" *Washington Quarterly* (Autumn 1981):8.

16. Major General Richard X. Larkin and Edward M. Collins, Defense Intelligence Agency, statement before the Joint Economic Committee, Subcommittee on International Trade, Finance and Security Economics, *Allocation of Resources in the Soviet Union and China-1981,* July 8, 1981, p. 48. The study notes that if "the line is amortized in 8 years, about $2 billion would be required for interest and principal reduction, leaving $5 billion in hard currency earnings" (p. 48).

17. Ray Dafter, "U.S. Bid to Offset Soviet Gas Imports to Europe," *Financial Times,* April 23, 1982, p. 4. The study, written by Energy Advice, is entitled "Alternative Strategies for Natural Gas in Western Europe."

18. Boyce I. Greer, "Soviet Natural Gas Exports and West European Security: The Yamburg Natural Gas Pipeline" (unpublished manuscript, Harvard University, June 23, 1981), p. 7.

19. Ibid., p. 18.

20. Steve McTiernan, *The Petroleum Situation* (New York: Chase Manhattan Bank Energy Economics Division, October 1981), p. 2.

21. "Europeans Eye Domestic Gas Fields for Strategic Buffer," *Petroleum Intelligence Weekly,* May 10, 1982, pp. 4-5.

5 Soviet Energy Development as an Issue in Alliance Strategy

Western strategy toward the CMEA needs to be reformulated within a more-comprehensive framework. The CoCom meetings and allied economic forums are significant vehicles, which hold the potential to contribute greatly to the common defense. CoCom in particular should be just as important as defense ministerial meetings, for strategic trade issues affect alliance cohesion and security as do purely military issues. The alliance must jointly decide if an economically sound and solvent Soviet bloc as net energy exporters is in the West's long-term strategic interest as net energy importers. It makes no sense to announce that the allies have agreed not to undercut each other's sanctions (as was done during the CoCom deliberations of January 1982) when the lack of a unified response constitutes just such a breach.

In this context, the Siberian pipeline poses special difficulties for the North Atlantic community. The project is fated to symbolize transatlantic discord and disunity and will build upon the current drift in allied perspectives, which could threaten the foundations upon which the alliance was built.

Irrespective of Moscow's long-range objectives when the project was first proposed, Soviet foreign policy and economic goals can only be advanced by completion of the pipeline, if for no other reason than the damage already engendered by intra-alliance quarreling over this one issue. Definitions, priorities, and objectives must be frankly debated, or NATO will be doomed to continual misunderstanding and frustration. Lacking political cohesion, it will be difficult to retain an effective and credible security posture. Soviet pressure, both military and political, will be maintained on Western Europe, pressure that contributed to the popular sentiment calling for greater accommodation with the Soviet Union precisely because it is so powerful. As a contributing element to the withering of trust and accord between allies, the Siberian pipeline and the divergent symbolism attached to it provides an early example of the serious problems facing the NATO alliance in the 1980s.

The Siberian pipeline and the extension of Western credits to the Soviet bloc raise important questions that extend beyond the ordinary purview of alliance concerns. NATO is usually characterized as best suited to grapple with military deterrence and defense and, perhaps, political integration; economic affairs (in theory and practice) are more often than not relegated to the annual summits or OECD's permanent committees.

The continuation of this approach virtually guarantees that issues cutting across traditional categories or intimately connected with alliance security yet originating outside formal NATO delimitations (as defined in Article 6 of the North Atlantic Treaty) will not receive timely or coordinated attention. The NATO Economics Directorate is an underutilized asset uniquely situated within the organization. As part of an overtly defense-oriented bureaucracy, the Economics Directorate is best able to undertake strategic trade and energy studies as they relate to the military security of the alliance. Institutionalization of annual policy-planning sessions at the ministerial level—by the respective ministers of trade or commerce—would be specifically charged with reviewing alliance progress in these areas, as is now done in strictly military issues through the routinized meetings of the NATO defense ministers.

A number of issues requiring further study are highly relevant in relation to Soviet energy development:

1. Soviet strategy in Third World oil diplomacy.
2. Soviet proposals for an extensive East-West (European) electricity grid.
3. Quantification of the economic and military effectiveness of technology transfer into the Soviet bloc.
4. Soviet foreign and military policies in the Persian Gulf region and the relationship between these policies and energy problems in the CMEA.
5. Soviet and East European energy demand structures and the success or failure of CMEA conservation programs over time.

Common military strategies directed toward ensuring a stable deterrence have proved their utility through thirty years of alliance development. Strategic trade concerns have recently surfaced as a vital component of allied strength, both military and political. Movement toward common strategic trade strategies must be viewed as part of a necessary alliance process—a process that seeks to integrate the disparate elements of allied power that together comprise Western sucurity.

Of these five major security issues raised as worthy of further allied study, among the most vexing has been intra-NATO disputes over Soviet strategy in the Persian Gulf. The problems posed by energy-induced Soviet action in the Persian Gulf are particularly difficult for NATO because of the extra-Atlantic nature of the relevant contingencies.

Concern over Soviet strategy in this extremely important region has been sharpened since the invasion of Afghanistan in December 1979. The series of pessimistic CIA reports beginning in 1977, detailing the rapid decline of Soviet oil production, fed allied fears of an imminent Soviet march into the Persian Gulf states, principally into Iran.

President Carter responded in his 1980 State of the Union address with a declaration of intent to protect the oil-producing states and the westward flow of oil from external interference. The coincidence of projected Soviet bloc oil shortages with the intervention in Afghanistan caused allied leaders to focus attention on Soviet intentions and opportunities in the Persian Gulf.

Yet NATO's response was divided. The Carter administration began planning a rapid deployment force, while the European allies generally feared that such an interventionist force would result in greater Arab mistrust of the West. Chancellor Schmidt, for example, did not believe that the Soviet invasion of Afghanistan necessarily helped Soviet military power. Collective NATO action therefore would be counterproductive.

Within the alliance, two major schools of thought concerning Soviet regional intentions compete for ascendancy. The first may be referred to as the expansionist school. Adherents cite the steady growth since 1964 of real Soviet defense expenditures, particularly for procurement of hardware, and past Soviet or proxy military expeditions ranging from Angola to Afghanistan. These military excursions are of an offensive, not defensive, nature. Viewing the USSR as a modified extension of the czarist imperial tradition, with an ever-expanding definition of security resulting in opportunistic expansionism, the expansionists foresee an aggressive Soviet move into the Persian Gulf region precipitated by major energy shortfalls in the Soviet bloc. Transfer of energy-related technologies, as asserted by Secretary of Defense Caspar Weinberger, would only strengthen the Soviet economy while failing to minimize Soviet interest in domination or control of the Persian Gulf region.

The second school of thought relies on optimistic analyses, which call for steady growth in Soviet hydrocarbon supply. Having removed the alleged impetus for Soviet military action in the Persian Gulf, this group sees superpower competition in the northwest Indian Ocean and Persian Gulf regions limited to political conflict set against a backdrop of naval maneuvering. Energy-technology trade with the Soviet Union is seen as increasing world oil and gas supplies while simultaneously offering the Soviet Union significant incentives for refraining from direct military assault.

Both of these approaches have problems. The expansionists imply that the Soviet Union does not accept either extended deterrence or uncontrollable escalation, despite vocal Soviet protestations following President Carter's (and subsequent officials') declaration of the willingness to use military force to defend the unimpeded flow of Persian Gulf oil. A direct Soviet military thrust does not appear likely precisely because Moscow cannot be assured of a limited U.S. response—that is, a response limited by the type of weapons and the particular theater of operations chosen by the USSR.

Those who believe the Soviet Union will not attack Western interests in the Persian Gulf because Soviet oil supply will be sufficient ignore the enormous windfall in escalated oil prices (which would redound to Soviet benefit as an exporter of oil) emanating from an alteration of the gulf's status quo. A political change in one or more of the key gulf oil-producing states, achieved either directly or covertly, would send shock waves through world financial and oil markets.

Similarly, European proponents of the Siberian natural-gas pipeline to Western Europe have argued that Soviet hard currency and possibly East European energy requirements will be fulfilled with the pipeline's planned completion in 1984, thereby obviating any energy-induced Soviet necessity to move militarily or covertly in the Persian Gulf. U.S. policy pronouncements have been faulted for claiming that, on the one hand, a looming energy crisis could drive Moscow to seek control over Persian Gulf oil supplies, while on the other hand, the rapid development and distribution of the abundant West Siberian natural-gas reserves will enable Moscow to ensnare Western Europe in a dangerously asymmetrical energy relationship.

Does the argument necessarily hold? Oil shortfalls and natural-gas surpluses in the West Siberian basin are not mutually exclusive items on the Soviet policy agenda. Natural-gas utilization in the Soviet bloc can only partially substitute for declining oil supplies, and exports will not now earn as much hard currency in the mid-1980s as Moscow had earlier planned. Oil exports to the West at 1981 levels would earn more hard currency than would natural-gas exports through the new pipeline in 1985. An oil-export strategy is clearly preferred but not seen as viable in the longer term—hence the gas-pipeline project.

Soviet diversion of 1 to 2 mmbd of Persian Gulf oil, accomplished through indirect or coercive means for additional CMEA consumption, would be difficult grounds for Western Europe to cancel pipeline-related technical assistance. The need for new European imports of natural gas has been clearly established and reiterated by goverment statements. After the pipeline has been built, Western Europe stands to lose its entire investment by refusing to accept Soviet gas imports.

Alternatively Soviet-sponsored maritime terrorism in the Persian Gulf could drive supertanker insurance rates or spot-oil prices high enough so that dwindling Soviet oil exports would realize greater earnings. A surge in world oil prices would additionally boost the floor price of natural-gas exports to Western Europe because the new Siberian gas-export contracts contain price escalators tied to price changes in a competing fuels mix consisting of various crudes and refined products.

The Persian Gulf is important to the USSR because it is important to the Western alliance system. Limited actions, especially those that are difficult to trace with any certainty, may hold great appeal to Moscow in the next few years while there is still Soviet oil available for export. Aggravating NATO's political and resource difficulties in the region cannot be dismissed out of hand and can, in fact, be regarded as a plausible concomitant to Soviet measures to secure West European participation in and dependence on Siberian natural-gas development.

The interrelationships of issues make any long-range analysis difficult and, because of the many complexities and uncertainties, raise as many questions as are answered. Early inquiry is essential if the West is to understand better the nature of the Soviet energy-political problem and so devise wise, prudent, and coordinated policies.

Index

About the Author

Jonathan B. Stein joined the staff of the Center for Strategic and International Studies in August 1981. He is currently research associate in energy studies, with particular focus on Soviet energy and alliance relations, Arctic resource development, and OPEC and emergency planning.

Mr. Stein received the B.A. from Vassar College in 1979 and was awarded a Vassar Fellowship for graduate study in international relations. He received the M.S. in foreign service from Georgetown University School of Foreign Service in 1981, with a concentration in international energy and resources and a strong minor in international security affairs.

Before joining the center, Mr. Stein worked as a federal summer intern in the directorate of European and NATO Affairs, Office of International Security Affairs, at the Department of Defense. He served as country desk officer for the Soviet Union and the Warsaw Pact states. His work included analysis of Soviet energy problems, U.S.-Soviet relations since the Soviet intervention in Afghanistan, and Soviet-bloc political and military issues.